From Dropout to Achiever

By Youth Communication

Edited by Al Desetta

Read. Write. Succeed.

From Dropout to Achiever

Executive Editors
Keith Hefner and Laura Longhine

Contributing Editors
Nora McCarthy, Andrea Estepa, Tamar Rothenberg, Rachel Blustain, Philip Kay, Kendra Hurley, and Autumn Spanne

Layout & Design
Efrain Reyes, Jr. and Jeff Faerber

Cover Photo Illustration
Joanne Pendola

Copyright © 2012 by Youth Communication®

All rights reserved under International and Pan-American Copyright Conventions. Unless otherwise noted, no part of this book may be reproduced, stored in a retrieval system, or transmitted in any form or by any means, electronic, mechanical, photocopying, recording, or otherwise, without express written permission of the publisher, except for brief quotations or critical reviews.

For reprint information, please contact Youth Communication.

ISBN 978-0-9661256-1-0

Third, Expanded Edition
The first edition of this book was entitled *From Dropout to Dreamer*.

Printed in the United States of America

Youth Communication®
New York, New York
www.youthcomm.org

Table of Contents

Hiding My Talent No More, *Jesselin Rodriguez* 11
    Jesselin does poorly in junior high, until a friend tells her she may lose the chance to go to college.

From Inmate to College Student, *Marlo Scott* 16
    Marlo's lust for money gets him in trouble, but he learns to redirect that desire into a plan to become an accountant.

A Stranger in a Strange School, *Esther Rajavelu* 22
    Esther's first day in 8th grade is a nervewracking one: she's a newly-arrived immigrant, and her classmates seem "weird."

Will the Tortoise Win the Race?, *Eric Green* 27
    A learning disability and the difficulties of living in care have caused Eric to fall far behind in high school.

Picking Myself Up, *Anita Ames* 33
    Anita hates the rules at her Catholic school, but soon realizes it's hard to stay on track without them.

Afraid to Learn, *Omar Morales* 39
    Omar has trouble concentrating because he gets picked on by the other kids.

Sticking With Your 'Own Kind,' *Cassandra Thadal* 44
    Cassandra's high school is diverse, but students rarely mix in the cafeteria.

Contents

Getting Guys Off My Back, *Artiqua Steed* 49
    Artiqua faces sexual harrasment at school.

Black Girl, White School, *Angelina Darrisaw* 53
    Angelina feels out of place at her elite private school.

Dropout Blues, *Diana Moreno* 59
    *Diana is a bookworm in the early grades but drops out
    when she gets to high school.*

When Great Isn't Good Enough, *Janill Briones* 66
    *Janill's mother is never satisfied with her
    accomplishments.*

They Called Me a 'Crack Baby,' *Antwaun Garcia* 71
    *When students discover he can't read, Antwaun is
    teased and called a "crack baby."*

The Suburbs: A Different World, *Dean Torres* 74
    *When Dean visits a suburban high school he is shocked
    to discover clean and quiet classrooms, and a lot of
    learning going on.*

Real Smart, *Amber Grof* 79
    *Amber gets into a special high school where she can
    earn both a diploma and a two-year college degree, but
    she has trouble handling the workload.*

A School Where I Can Be Myself, *Wilber Valenzuela* 86
    Wilber finds acceptance at a high school for gay youth.

Contents

No More Hand Holding, *Edgar Lopez* 90
    A college visit is a wake up call for Egdar, who realizes that to succeed he will have to to take more responsibility for himself.

How I Graduated, *Angi Baptiste* 96
    A sense of failure holds Angi back in school, until she breaks the pattern and gets help.

Lost in a Big School, *Danica Webb* 101
    Danica's big school is staffed by rude security guards, distracted teachers, and a bad guidance counselor. She falls behind.

What's Wrong With Reading? *Anthony Turner* 106
    Anthony is teased when his classmates catch him reading a book for fun, but he refuses to change his ways.

You're On Your Own, Kid, *Otis Hampton* 111
    Otis has a difficult time adjusting to college his freshman year.

FICTION SPECIAL: Schooled, *Paul Langan* 117

Credits 126

About Youth Communication 127

About the Editors 128

More Helpful Books from Youth Communication 130

Introduction

For many teens, especially those from poor and distressed neighborhoods, success in school is a struggle. Graduating may involve overcoming family problems, bouncing back from a bad semester, dealing with a difficult foster family, or even dropping out for a time.

In the following true stories, teens write about challenges they've faced in school and how they've overcome them.

They form friendships they didn't expect, resist peer pressure, and persist in their studies despite setbacks and failure. They deal with sexual harassment, racial prejudice, and violence. They battle with the expectations of parents, peers, and teachers. They change schools and attitudes, but they never give up on achieving their goals.

The writers address a broad range of school experiences. As one of the few black students in a private school, Angelina is stereotyped. Omar's school makes it hard from him to concentrate in class. Cassandra, an immigrant from Haiti, wonders why students of different races and ethnic groups interact in the classroom, but then segregate themselves in the school cafeteria. Artiqua faces sexual harassment in the hallways until she confronts her tormentor. Antwaun overcomes the teasing of his classmates and learns to read and write.

Some writers, like Wilber Valenzuela in "A School Where I Can Be Myself" find support and a sense of community at smaller, alternative schools. Others find ways to succeed where they are. Jesselin neglects her studies in favor of making friends, before she realizes she may be sacrificing a college education and turns her performance around. Angi, who lives in foster care and has a history of abuse, manages to graduate from high school despite overwhelming odds.

These stories honor the struggles of teens for whom school

success is far from guaranteed.

In the following stories, names have been changed: *Picking Myself Up, Getting Guys Off My Back,* and *Lost in a Big School.*

Hiding My Talent No More

By Jesselin Rodriguez

When I was in elementary school, doing well in school was the only thing that mattered to me. I always thought that being the smartest meant being the best.

I got this idea because when my family used to ask me if I had done my homework and I told them "yes," they would say, "What a good little girl!" Every time they said something like that, it would go straight to my head. It made me feel like I was number one.

In my elementary school, a lot of kids seemed to share my attitude. It was common to see kids always wanting to do their best so that they could be teacher's pet. I would sometimes hear a teacher say to someone else, "Oh, this is so wonderful, you're the best student in the class, I've never had a problem with you." I wanted to hear a teacher say those things to me, too.

From Dropout to Achiever

When I got to junior high school, this all changed. The mood and the atmosphere of the school were totally different from what I was used to. I saw kids walking in and out of the building like nothing, hanging out in the auditorium when they did not belong there, and even screaming at teachers. There was a fight almost every day. No one seemed to care about their classes.

In that environment, you looked crazy if you were doing any work. The important thing was to have friends. If you didn't have any friends, then you were nothing. You would get picked on, cursed out in the hallways, and if you were to have a fight it would never be one-on-one. I decided schoolwork wasn't going to be my top priority anymore. Instead, I made it a point to have friends.

Instead of always going to class and doing my homework, like I had in elementary school, I got into a new routine. I started thinking of school as a playground. It was like I could do anything there—cut class, write on the walls, hide in the bathrooms—and nobody would know about it because there were so many kids in that school.

When I did go to class, I'd walk in 20 minutes late, sit with a friend, and talk the rest of the period away. When the teachers would ask me why I was late, I'd tell them that I was in the bathroom or that I was talking to another teacher about something. They wouldn't really bother me after that.

This doesn't mean that I never did any work. I did just enough to pass. But I never let my friends find out. On the days when I did my homework, I used to wait until after the class to give it to the teacher so my friends wouldn't see. If they knew, I was sure they would give me a hard time. They would be like, "What are you doing the work for? What, you think you're better than us?"

I've always cared about what other people thought. In elementary school I was liked and respected for being smart and always doing my work—not just by my family and the teachers, but by the other kids too. But in junior high, I thought my classmates would like me better if I acted more like them—lazy and not caring about anything except going home to watch TV.

After pretending to be lazy for a while, I started to actually get lazy. By January of 6th grade, I hated school. I hated the fact that I had to get up so early. I hated to do my homework. After class, I just wanted to go to my bed and sleep or watch TV. The less work I did, the harder it got to do any work at all.

A lot of my teachers said that I had the potential to get high marks if I spent more time in class and got rid of my friends.

> *In junior high, I thought my classmates would like me better if I acted more like them—lazy and not caring about anything.*

But I didn't listen. I thought that they were just saying that. I didn't think that they really cared. When I brought my report card home, my mom would say, "I know you can do better; next time I want this to be higher." I didn't listen to her either.

Then something happened. My class was divided up. The kids with the worst behavior and grades, including most of my friends, were sent to a different building. Since I didn't have my crew to do things with anymore, I felt I had two choices—I could either not go to school at all, or I could start doing my work.

I knew my mother would kill me if she ever heard me say anything about not going to school. So I started to go to class every day and began to do my homework on a more regular basis. My teachers were happy and, inside, so was I.

By the time I was in 8th grade (my last year in junior high), I had worked my way up to a 'B' average. I still felt that I could do better, but I didn't want to get higher grades than most of the people in my class. I thought that they would get mad at me and be like, "Oh, now she thinks that she's smarter than me."

Then came 9th grade and a big reality check. I had thought that high school was going be the same as junior high, only more so—a bigger playground to roam in. I was wrong. Even though most of the kids were the same, the atmosphere was very different.

You see, my high school had been closed and several new, smaller schools had been started to replace it. My new school was so small that there were only about 50 students in the whole place. There was no chance to run around because every teacher knew who you were and where you were supposed to be every minute of the day.

My teachers knew that I was smart and saw right through my front of acting like I didn't care. Still, I thought that as long as I handed in a couple of pieces of work where I did my best, they would be satisfied and not bother me all the time. But they wouldn't leave me alone. For my whole freshman year, I was constantly told that I could do better. It just went in one ear and came out the other.

It had been my dream to be the first one in my family to go to college. Now I realized I had to work to make that dream come true.

Then, over the summer, I was talking to a friend of mine who was in college. My friend started telling me that there was no way I would get a scholarship the way I was going. Then he told me that I should probably just forget about college because it seemed like I would never even be able to finish high school if I was so lazy.

He put so much fear in me that I spent the rest of that summer thinking about what he said. It was the same thing my teachers had been telling me for years. It finally started to sink in. For a long time, it had been my dream to be the first one in my family to graduate from high school and go to college. Now I realized that I was going to have to work to make that dream come true.

A week before school started, I promised myself that I was going to bring my grades up till they could not get any higher. And that's exactly what I did.

For my whole 10th grade year, I did nothing but work. I used to be in school from 8:00 in the morning until 5:30 or 6 in the evening. I did so well that most people were like, "I knew you had it in you, but I didn't realize how much."

I was staying after school so much that my adviser started to worry about me. The principal even started kicking me out because I was there really late practically every day. (I could never figure out why they were complaining about my staying after school. I thought that was a good thing.)

Breaking my lazy habits wasn't easy. In fact, I think it was the hardest thing I have ever done. I had to get used to doing my homework every night, not just when I felt like it. And I had to make a lot of sacrifices. I could not sit home and watch TV all day. I hardly listened to the radio.

And I didn't see a lot of my old friends outside of school. Every time they'd say, "Jesse, let's go downtown so I can go buy this shirt," or, "Let's go downtown and just chill," I was always saying, "No, I can't, I have to stay after school and finish my work."

I've made a lot of new friends since junior high and I think they're part of the reason why I've been able to change. Because of them, I don't worry so much anymore about what other people will think of me if I get good marks. They accept me the way I am. If they don't see me studying, they will be like, "Why aren't you doing any work? That's not like you. You better hurry up, this is due Friday." That makes me feel good. Because they really care, they want to see me work.

So, here I am, a junior almost ready for college—not at all ashamed of how bright I am, and not caring who knows it. It feels like that good girl I once had inside me has come back.

Jesselin wrote this story when she was 16. She graduated from high school and went on to Hampshire College.

From Inmate to College Student

By Marlo Scott

Throughout my life, my family has always been in financial crisis.

My mother died of cancer when I was 11, and after that, there was even less money for my father to take care of my brother and me.

When I was 13, my father, brother, and I lived in a homeless shelter. My father eventually found an apartment in Queens, New York, but there were still nights I had nothing to eat.

In middle school, things stabilized, but I noticed that other kids had nicer clothes than I did. I felt inadequate, and I felt different because my mother had died. I made up for it by being smart. All the cool kids who dressed nice came to me for help in class. This made me feel good about myself, and gave me a reason to excel in school. My mother had always told me that life is hard without an education and encouraged me to do well in school.

In freshman algebra, when I realized I was good in math, I decided I wanted to be an accountant. I figured I would apply my math skills to real-life situations. I wanted to help people manage their money and invest to make more. In addition, an average CPA salary is $65,000 per year. Knowing that I could make plenty of money doing something I enjoyed sparked my dream and kept me focused on school, particularly math.

> **I was supposed to be graduating in June, but now I had screwed all that up.**

However, after I turned 15, I did not want to keep going without the nice things my classmates had. The weekly allowance of $5 my father gave me wasn't enough to buy the expensive things I wanted, like Nike sneakers.

Maybe because I had to grow up without the nourishment of motherly love, I badly wanted nice clothes and money. The girls in high school liked the boys with that luxury. One girl named Lynda turned me down after she saw me with a pair of cheap sneakers. She simply laughed when I asked her out, and the next day I saw her with a boy who was wearing expensive Jordans.

I continued to do well academically, but I missed my mother and I began to fight a lot. Anger and jealousy toward kids with nice things built up within me.

When I was 15, I stole a Play Station Handheld from a kid on the subway platform, and got caught. As punishment, family court sent me to a residential treatment facility (RTC) in upstate New York. After serving 12 months, the RTC, Graham Windham, discharged me from living on their campus. I decided to remain at the school there as a day student. I took a train up every day from my father's house in Queens. At Graham, I could finish high school in three years instead of four. I could also focus more because the classes were smaller.

Though I received abundant help from many supportive staff members at Graham, I remained emotionally damaged. I still wanted to dress nicer than I could afford.

I also felt angry because I was a good kid, but I never felt any recognition for my hard work in school. My mother used to go out and buy me whatever I wanted whenever she noticed me improving and excelling in school. So I missed her whenever I got a good grade.

All the anger and jealousy led me to do more rebellious things, one of which landed me in jail for four months. I would rather not go into the details, but it was grand larceny, and I was remanded to Riker's Island prison.

When I first reached Riker's, it was December 2010. I was supposed to be finishing my senior year at Graham and graduating in June, but now I had screwed all that up. I had no idea when I would be going back home because my sentencing date was not until April 2011. Therefore, I entered a GED program in Riker's.

The program required you to take three classes: math, English, and writing. Because I was 16, I was in an adolescent classroom. Guest speakers often spoke to us about school outside of jail. They wanted to encourage inmates to go back to school following their release.

Sometimes I did not even want to listen. When I heard their speeches feelings of guilt and regret about being arrested, and possibly forfeiting my chance to enter college early would rise within me. I would get angry and sometimes talk loudly during class or pick on kids who were new. When I disrupted the class, the corrections officers supervising the students removed me from class and placed me in isolation—a small, square room with no window. Being there was lonely and boring, and it made the day go by even more slowly.

I began thinking about how I could avoid ever sitting in prison again. The answer was patience, which, ironically, I gained from spending four months in a cell. I had to wait on the corrections officers for everything at Rikers. I had to wait for chow, I had to wait for the GED program, and I had to wait for TV time. Over time, I got used to it. That's when I realized, no matter how hard things get, I always have something to go after. As long as I keep doing well in school, I always have a greater future to seek.

My time in the prison's GED program also gave me a chance to expand my vocabulary. The reading and writing classes gave us SAT-based passages and comprehension questions, which built on the work I had been doing at Graham.

In April, I got the good news that my sentence was four months jail time and five years probation. I had already served almost four months, so I'd be free in a few weeks. My lawyer told me my sentence was short in part because I had done so well at Graham. I had told the judge that I wanted to finish high school at Graham and get a real diploma, and she liked that.

When I arrived back at Graham I felt like a young child impatient for Christmas. When I finally sat in my normal classroom again, I ripped open every book as if it were a present.

Studying while incarcerated had been easy because it made time go faster. Back home, I stayed in the habit and studied U.S. history, chemistry, and English for hours every night. (Those are the topics covered in the Regents exams, which you need to graduate in New York.) I worried I might not graduate on time, and then regretted, again, the mistake that had landed me in Riker's. But this time, I used those feelings to make me work harder.

All my hard work paid off. I earned a 75 in both chemistry and English and an 89 on the U.S. history Regents test. I graduated in June 2011, and I felt so proud.

Since I missed those months of school, I was late applying to college. In May 2011, a month after leaving prison, I enrolled for the fall semester in a community college in upstate New York, 164 miles away. Dorm housing was limited and the school placed me on a waiting list. Three weeks before the fall semester started, the school notified me that no dorm rooms had opened up and might not until October. I obviously could not commute 164 miles, so I withdrew from classes.

Dropping those classes made my goal of graduating college feel further away, but I applied for the spring semester at another school outside the city. I took the long train ride up there seven times to ensure my enrollment. I interviewed there in December, and two weeks later, I got a letter. I opened it full of hope, but the letter said that the college would not admit me because I was on probation. My probation officer has to visit my residence every month, and they did not want a probation officer in their dorms.

> **As long as I keep doing well in school, I always have a greater future to seek.**

I felt despair, desperation, and more guilt at how I had messed up. But that very week, my father told me about a college in New York City known for its business and criminal justice programs. Although my father has been by my side supporting me, I did not expect him to know about a school, especially a business college. He has not attended school since the 11th grade. However, his friend at work has a daughter that attends this school and told him about it. The school's admissions materials say that 90% of their 2010 graduates now have full-time jobs.

As I began the admissions process at this third college, I felt much more confident due to my experience at the previous two schools. I'd gotten comfortable filling out all the enrollment, housing, and financial aid paperwork, and I understood the process. Plus, I got outstanding scores on the admissions test and got enough financial aid to afford school without having to get a job. My good scores also allowed me to start two months before the actual semester with condensed classes that award credits in a shorter time than regular-semester classes.

As I finally close in on my college dreams, I try not to let things get to me easily anymore. I've learned to worry less about my social status amongst my peers or what I'm wearing. It helps that I have a future to look forward to now.

The fact that I went from a jail cell to college in one year makes me proud and confident that I will do well in college and become an accountant. The road to college was not easy. A lot of studying enabled me to graduate high school early, despite four months of incarceration. In addition, my desire to be financially independent and to have the things I want helps me focus on my success. I still want the nice clothes, but I can wait to buy them with my accountant's salary.

My good grades have remained my salvation through all my wrongdoings. I could have avoided jail by simply staying patient and waiting for my gratification. Instead, I departed from my road to success a couple times—and I was lucky that the judge appreciated my school achievements. I feel blessed and lucky to realign with my path toward becoming a CPA.

After graduating from high school, Marlo enrolled in college and is enjoying it very much.

A Stranger in a Strange School

By Esther Rajavelu

I was really nervous about my first day of 8th grade, not just because I was a new student, but because I was also a new immigrant to the United States.

As I looked around at the other students in my school, I felt like I was the only person who was "normal."

I saw a skinny boy with pale skin, light blond hair cut close to his scalp, and the bluest eyes I had ever seen. I thought he was the weirdest looking person alive.

Then I glanced at a girl with long black hair like my own, but her skin was lighter and yellower than my dark brown complexion. I noticed her eyes. They were tiny, black, and at first I though she was squinting. I had no idea that people could look like that. I thought that everyone would look like me.

Finally, the teacher came and opened the classroom. I stood

outside the door uncertain whether to go in and sit with all those weird kids, or to turn around and run home as fast as my feet would carry me. Then I remembered what my dad had told me that morning: "You have to study as hard as you can, actually even more. That's the only way you'll ever be successful."

I knew I couldn't study very hard if I didn't even enter the class, so I took my first steps towards my education in the United States.

I didn't know where to sit, so I stood looking for a friendly face. When I didn't find one, I just walked straight to the last seat in the last row.

As the teacher took attendance, I noticed two Indian names being called. I craned my neck to see where they were sitting and caught a glimpse of their backs. Nothing made me happier than knowing that there were people in my class as "normal" as me. I looked forward to getting to know them. I thought we would be great friends, because we were all from India.

The teacher gave everyone a program card. When she was finished, she said, "Go to your next class."

Everybody got up and walked out. I looked at my card. There were some codes and

As I looked around at the other students, I felt like I was the only person who was "normal."

numbers printed on it, but I didn't know what they stood for. I sat in my seat wondering what to do next. When I saw some new kids come into the room, I got really worried.

Another teacher walked in, and ordered everyone to take a seat. He finished taking attendance and said, "Is there anyone whose name I haven't called?"

He hadn't called my name, but by now I was scared out of my wits. I knew I didn't belong in this class, and if I called attention to myself by answering his question all the kids in the class would start laughing.

From Dropout to Achiever

Now I felt that I was the "weird" one and everyone else in the room was "normal." After all, they knew what was going on, but I had no hint about what to do.

I decided to pretend that everything was alright and sit as still as possible. Unfortunately, the teacher noticed me and said, "Hey, you in the last seat, did I call your name?"

I wanted to lie, but when I opened my mouth I said, "No."

"What's your name?" he asked.

"Esther," I said.

"Your last name?" he asked.

"Rajavelu."

"How do you spell it?"

"R-A-J-A-V-E-L-U," I said.

By now, all the kids had turned around and were staring at me. I was so embarrassed. All the confident feelings I had when I left my house were gone.

The teacher searched the sheet he had in his hand. "I don't see your name here," he said.

I already knew he wouldn't see my name, but I didn't know what to say. He asked for my program card.

"You don't belong in this class," he said.

I knew that too. I looked down at my hands.

"You have to go to room 410," he said. "You better hurry before the teacher marks you absent."

Without any warning I started crying. At first the teacher looked shocked, but then asked in a kinder tone, "Are you new to this school?"

"Yes," I mumbled.

He told me to take my bag and go to room 410 and he gave me a note explaining why I was late. I walked to the door with tears running down my cheeks, while the whole class stared.

At the door, I turned around and asked in a shaky voice, "How do you get to room 410?"

Matter of factly, the teacher turned to a boy in the front row. "Will you take this young lady to her class," he asked him.

A Stranger in a Strange School

I followed the boy, who was short with a red face (I'll call him William). I thought it was so nice of him to walk me to class. As we walked down the hall, I wanted to let him know he was the only friend I had in the whole school. I was just about to open my mouth, when another boy waved to him.

William pointed to me and said something to his friend. I couldn't understand because it sounded different than the English I knew. They looked at me and laughed. I swallowed my thanks and stifled a new set of tears.

Finally, William left me at my new class, and I went in. I was so nervous. I would have given anything to go back home. I wanted to be safe with people I knew, not be stuck here with all these strangers.

I showed the new teacher the note and he asked me to come in.

"Sit down," he said, pointing to an empty seat in the middle of the room. I noticed that the Indian girl from my homeroom was sitting next to me.

She smiled. She was the first person to smile at me that day. I was relieved that she was sitting right next to me.

I walked to the door with tears running down my cheeks, while the whole class stared.

After class, we talked and I found out that we had most of our classes together. During lunch she took me to the cafeteria. We got our lunch and walked to a table where her friends sat.

"This is Esther," said my new friend. "She's new to this school."

They smiled and said hello and started asking me questions.

"Where did you go to school before?" asked another Indian girl.

"I went to school in India."

"Wow, so you just got here," said a white girl with braces.

"Yes."

From Dropout to Achiever

"So how come you know English?" asked a Chinese girl.

I didn't understand what knowing English had to do with coming from India. I had spoken English since I was a little kid.

"My parents taught me," I said, just to be polite.

"You have a British accent," said another girl sitting at the far end of the table (at the time, I didn't speak like an American). "Have you ever been to England?"

I thought it was odd for her to say that I had an accent. After all, they were the ones who sounded strange.

"No, I've never been to England," I said.

Then they all started talking about their teachers, classes, the "school nerds," and all the cute guys in 8th grade. It was both the same and different from a conversation I would have had with friends in India. In India we spoke about teachers, classes, and "smart kids." But we never talked about guys.

This group was friendlier than I had expected and I began to feel at ease. I started the day thinking all these kids looked so strange and there I was eating my lunch, hoping they would be my friends.

On the first day I walked into school, my mind was filled with prejudices about my "normalcy" and their "weirdness." After five years of going to school in America, I now feel that "normal" comes very close to "weird," because who's to say what's normal and what's weird?

On that first day in school, if I could have seen myself the way I am now—with short skirts, eyeliner, and dark lipstick—I would have thought I was weird, too.

Esther was 17 when she wrote this story. She later graduated from Wesleyan University and earned a graduate degree from the Wharton School of Business at the University of Pennsylvania.

Will the Tortoise Win the Race?

By Eric Green

Everybody says you need to graduate from high school to succeed in life. But what if you just can't pass your classes? Should you keep trying? I'm 20 years old and I'm still in the 11th grade. I failed 9th grade once and failed 10th grade three times. I'm not sure I'll ever graduate.

Until 9th grade, I was in special education classes. In elementary school, I felt like the smartest kid in the class. I was a straight A student. In junior high, I constantly got 100s on spelling quizzes, and sometimes made the honor roll.

In 6th grade, I started to have trouble for the first time. When my math teacher called me up to the board to solve a problem, I was the slowest one to finish in the whole class. Some of my teachers yelled and screamed at me. One teacher called me "slow" and "stupid." I began to hate her and think of myself as stupid. On good days, I'd tell myself, "I'm smart, just not as quick as other people."

In the 9th grade, I got switched to regular classes and went to the resource room for extra help. In my regular classes, students talked down to kids in special ed., calling us slow. I'd think, "That's where you're wrong. I go to resource room because I have a learning disability, and I'm willing to get as much help as possible." But I kept my mouth shut because I didn't want to get teased even more.

That year, my biological mom died. My mind was not on school at all. Suddenly school was too hard. I seemed to have lost my ability to understand the work. I began to think I was not intelligent enough to pass high school classes. I would sit in class looking at the assignment while everyone else completed theirs.

I felt that some of my teachers did not want to deal with me anymore. Eventually, I stopped asking for help.

Sometimes when I took an assignment seriously I'd do well. Then I'd feel proud and confident. Most of the time, though, I'd become overwhelmed and frustrated.

Once, in math class, I got extra help and did all of my assignments. When I got my report card, I saw that my math teacher had given me a 65.

"Why did you give me a 65?" I asked him.

"You didn't do well on the exams," he said.

I was furious. Didn't he know I was working as hard as I could? Didn't he understand how it feels to try hard but not be rewarded or recognized? I thought I deserved a better grade because of my effort, even if I couldn't do well on the tests.

Situations like that made me feel neglected by my teachers. Growing up, my parents and my first foster parent neglected me.

My biological parents would disappear without a trace and leave my siblings and me in the house for hours. They didn't seem to notice who I was or what I needed.

I felt the same way when my teachers overlooked the efforts I made, or stood by while other kids in the class teased me and called me names. I felt that some of my teachers did not want to deal with me anymore and didn't pay attention to me when I asked for help. I felt lonely and isolated and stuck with problems that I couldn't solve.

Eventually, I stopped asking for help. I'd feel stupid any time I tried to complete a difficult task. I stopped believing that I could ever pass, even if I got all the extra help in the world. I thought I'd never be a successful person.

Then I began to refuse to do classwork. I'd spend my time writing poems or drawing pictures—two things I know I'm good at. When the teacher asked me about the assignment I was supposed to be doing, I'd have nothing to show.

I hoped that my teachers would notice that I was angry, or lost. But when I took my adoptive mother, Lorine, to my parent-teacher conferences, my teachers only seemed frustrated.

One teacher told her, "Eric is a very talented poet and artist, but he doesn't do the work that is required of him. He just sits in the back of the classroom and writes his poems. He is very inattentive and uncooperative. He's a nice young man. I know he can do better."

Lorine said, "You see, that's the same exact thing that I be telling him. He gets mad and starts to cop an attitude. He doesn't like to study, or do his homework. Every day he just comes home and sits on the floor and draws and writes poems."

Every teacher we met told my mother the same thing. Even my art teacher, whose class is my favorite, told her, "Eric is not paying attention in class, he does not do the assignments. Eric does what he wants to do."

From Dropout to Achiever

I felt embarrassed because it was the truth. One day in my art class, the task was to draw a still life of a bowl of fruit. While the rest of the class was drawing the fruit, I was doing my own drawings, because I only like to draw self-portraits, cartoon characters, and washing machines.

I knew that I should do what was asked of me instead of being troublesome. But when Lorine asked me why I wouldn't cooperate with my teachers, I was too embarrassed to come out with the reason for my behavior—that I felt like a failure. So I said, "I believe that school should suit my interests. I don't understand how learning math will help me become a poet or an artist!"

Finally, the anxiety and the feeling of wasting my life got to be too much. I told my mother, "I am dropping out."

"If you decide to drop out of high school, then you can leave this house and live with someone else," Lorine said.

> **My counselor explained to me that having a learning disability is different from being dumb.**

Luckily, my counselor helped me transfer to a smaller high school where I could get more attention. I thought that in a better environment I would do better in school and be able to go forward in life. At first, I was more focused and willing to do the work. The teachers went out of their way to help me, and the students were respectful and easy to get along with.

My counselor also explained to me that having a learning disability is different from being dumb. "When you're a smart person with a learning disability, you can master an academic curriculum if you have plenty of assistance and you work hard. A dumb person is one who is unwilling to participate in classes or stick to the curriculum," she said.

Lately, though, I've run into some new obstacles. In New York, you have to pass certain exams to graduate. I've taken some of those exams—in history and English—and I've failed all of them, some more than once.

And last year, I was looking through my file and I found out that I'd been diagnosed with Fetal Alcohol Syndrome. I looked that up on the internet and found out that it's a problem affecting children whose mothers drank a lot while they were pregnant. It listed these characteristics:

—difficulty getting along with friends and family
—mental retardation
—growth deficiencies
—behavior problems
—incomplete education

Looking at the list, I thought to myself, "Do those traits describe me? Is there something wrong with me?"

I felt depressed. I feared that I might never be a normal student and might never graduate from high school. I felt angry that my biological mother drank (I remember her drinking when I lived with her). I also worried that my brothers might have the same thing.

I went home and told Lorine what I had read and how I felt. She refused to believe it. She told me, "Eric, you're smart and you should not use that diagnosis as an excuse."

I also told some of my teachers, who told me, "You need to have confidence in your abilities. You have potential and the intelligence to succeed. You're smart, creative, artistic and unique. You write beautiful poetry. Do not punish yourself like that, Eric. Believe in yourself."

Right now, I'm not sure what to believe about myself. Some days I feel smart and hopeful, other days I'm discouraged. On those days, I don't even try to work toward graduation. I just sit in my classes, drawing and writing poetry. Those are my talents, and when I look at the words and pictures I've created, I feel like it doesn't matter if I succeed in high school or not.

Still, if I don't graduate, I'll feel like a fool for letting myself and my family and friends down. I'm a smart person, I want to succeed, and everybody's in my corner. My friends tell me, "Your mother is right to be upset with you. You need an education." My mom tells me, "I want to see you with that paper in your hand."

I want to see that, too.

Eric was 20 when he wrote this story. He succeeded in graduating from high school the following year.

Picking Myself Up

By Anita Ames

The day was hot but breezy and my cap and gown fit perfectly. Nothing was greater than the feeling of graduation. I'd been in the same school, Beginning With Children, from kindergarten through 8th grade. It was a small charter school where the principal, teachers, students and parents all knew each other. The day I graduated, I felt so accomplished. I had no idea that high school was another hurdle soon to come.

That night my mom and I sat down to dinner, and the steam from the mashed potatoes, baked chicken, corn bread and sweet peas hit my nose. I was about to dig in when I was rudely interrupted by my mom's voice. "Catherine McAuley HS has offered you a scholarship, so that's where you'll be going next year," she said. "The public school system will chew you up and spit you out."

From Dropout to Achiever

I was surprised. I had assumed I'd be going to Cobble Hill HS, a public high school in Brooklyn. I didn't want to go to private school. "I don't want to wear a uniform and have a whole bunch of girls in my face all day!" I said.

I knew my mom didn't want me to fall through the cracks and drop out like she had in her public high school. But I didn't care about the harsh realities of public school that she remembered, like fights every day and careless teachers. I wanted high school to be a choice that I made for myself. But my mom stuck to her decision.

That fall, private school hit me like a raging bull—fast and hard. The commute was an hour and a half and on the first day, the principal greeted all the freshmen in the auditorium with a prayer. Then we were given a conduct sheet and contract for our parents to sign.

I had no idea Catherine McAuley would be so strict and religious. I mean, I believed in God, but we prayed every morning in homeroom. That seemed excessive. There were a lot of unnecessary rules, too, like having to have your shirt tucked in and not having the tongue of your boot stick out of the uniform pants.

I hated wearing an ugly uniform. I hated going to an all-girls school where classmates who I thought were my friends talked about me behind my back. I also hated the hard work. Every day I had to bring home at least four textbooks. My mother told me things would get better and that I had to crawl before I walked. But I felt I would never be happy there.

Soon I met two friends at school who felt the same way. Sandra, Lori and I began taking out our anger by breaking all the rules, wearing our shirts any kind of way, even wearing sneakers. I hardly broke any rules at Beginning With Children because I loved making my principal there proud. But at McAuley I couldn't care less.

One day we all sat in our freshman English class taking notes. I was sick of paying attention, so I told Lori to throw a paper ball

Picking Myself Up

at Sandra, who was sleeping. Lori put smaller bits of paper into a larger piece to make the ball really hard, so it would definitely wake Sandra up.

But the ball missed Sandra and hit another girl, Jessica, who turned around and threw a ball at Lori. Then I threw a ball at Jessica and soon the entire class was having a paper ball fight. Everybody kept saying, "It hit me first," and "I didn't do anything." They never found out who started it.

When I started trouble like this in school, I felt powerful. I wanted to show that the administrators couldn't control my actions. So I kept doing it. My friends and I came to school late, had water fights in the bathroom and sang songs loudly during lunch. When the end of the school year came, Catherine McAuley's advisors sent a letter saying they didn't want me back. Although this hadn't been my plan, I was glad.

My mom, on the other hand, was disappointed that I'd lost my scholarship. She worried that I wouldn't finish high school if I went back to public school. But other private schools were too expensive without a scholarship, so she had no choice this time around.

Since I've always loved to write, I chose to attend the Secondary School for Journalism.

When I started trouble in school, I felt powerful. I wanted to show that the administrators couldn't control my actions.

It only had 630 students and I thought it couldn't be too bad. I imagined cute senior boys who played basketball, understanding teachers and no morning prayer.

The first day of school, I sat in the overcrowded lunchroom. People were throwing food, talking on their cell phones, listening to music—things that would never have been tolerated at Catherine McAuley. I was disgusted by the crushed food and spilled milk on the floor. But I still felt that anywhere was better than Catherine McAuley. Then a girl I'd met earlier that day came up to me and said, "I'm leaving. You coming to school tomorrow?"

"What do you mean you're leaving? We have four more periods left."

"I know. But I can just leave through the side door. The security guards won't say anything, especially if you're cool with them."

Cut out of school, just like that? It was too easy. The next day I saw the same girl in school looking calm, cool and collected. She didn't mention anything about getting in trouble. I felt all this freedom shouldn't go to waste. That afternoon, a boy showed me the side exit and I went home and slept the rest of the day. No one even realized I was gone.

Soon I found a cut buddy, a girl I met in the bathroom one day. We cut our 7th and 8th period gym class every day. Most of the time I would go to a friend's house to hang out. Other times I would just go home and crash. To me, this was the good life.

In the classes I did attend, I barely paid attention because I'd learned the same stuff as a freshman at Catherine McAuley. I began to realize that if I'd stayed there I would have learned a lot more, and that private school was strict for a reason: students were expected to succeed. I felt like the teachers at my public school didn't expect anything, because they'd gotten used to students who didn't make an effort. Maybe getting kicked out of private school wasn't so smart after all.

That realization hit me even harder at the end of the year, when I found out I had failed gym and would have to make up the credit in my senior year. I had done OK in my other classes, but I knew I could have done better.

Over the summer I thought about my education. My sister was home from her first year at college, and she told me that college was way more challenging than high school. It dawned on me that soon I would become a college student myself. Junior year was coming up and I knew it was important for college admissions. I had almost slipped through those cracks my mom warned me about, and I couldn't let myself become a failure and a statistic. I felt this was my last chance.

That fall I buckled down. I resisted the temptation to cut class by simply thinking about my cut buddy. We were still good friends, but she had dropped out of school. I started participating in different activities after school to keep myself busy and focused. I joined student council and started doing community service to get a sense of what I liked to do. I did work-readiness workshops at Henry Street Settlement, an after-school program, and began a writing internship at Youth Communication.

I struggled with math, so I made an appointment to get tutoring twice a week during my lunch period, which helped me feel more confident in math. I also began to read more books outside of class to enhance my vocabulary and prepare for the SATs. I read *To Kill a Mockingbird*, *The Catcher in the Rye* and anything else my English teacher told me was good. When I finished a book, my teacher and I would discuss it after class.

When I did my homework each night, I trained my mind to think beyond what I was reading and try to connect it with the world today. When we were studying the Progressive Era in U.S. History, for example, I saw that some of the support services that exist today, like Henry Street Settlement, were created during that time to help the struggling community.

I began to realize that private school was strict for a reason: students were expected to succeed.

One day I heard some people talking about honor roll. I never knew the school even had an honor roll, so I asked the secretary in the office where I could find it. "Right outside this office on the bulletin board," she said. The honor roll had names listed as gold (90+ average), silver (85-89 average) and bronze (80-84 average). When I saw my name, I felt proud, even though it was only on the bronze list.

From Dropout to Achiever

In private school, teachers always warned us that nobody cares about you in public school, that the students behave like animals and hardly anyone graduates. But I found only some of that was true. Yes, the students behaved like animals; yes, they disrespected teachers, but I couldn't agree with the "nobody cares" part.

It's true that no one stayed on my back about going to class, and when I cut school, no one called my house. But when I decided to ask for help, teachers were there for me. Once they saw I was trying, they gave me whatever help I needed. I realized that people do care, if you care about yourself.

I feel like I gave up too easily on private school when things got rough. I missed out on the better education that I would have received there. But in some ways I'm glad I switched. I ended up in the same place I think I would have ended up if I'd stayed at Catherine McAuley: starting college and ready to pursue a career in journalism. The difference is that in public school I've had to push myself more, as opposed to someone pushing me. I could've given up on public school just like I gave up on private school, but I didn't.

Now, as I start my freshman year at SUNY Albany (on a full scholarship!), I realize my switch helped prepare me for challenges that I may face in college. At such a large university, it's easy to get lost or fall off track. But since I've already had that experience, I know how to keep myself focused, ask for help when I need it, and ultimately stick things out. I can see how this skill will benefit me in college and in the world beyond.

Anita was 18 when she wrote this story. As she wrote in the story, she got a full scholarship to college.

Afraid to Learn

By Omar Morales

All my life I've been something of a loner and a sensitive kid. While other kids went out all the time, I was home listening to music, watching television, or just hanging out in front of the building where I live.

But my experience in school made me feel even more alone and made it hard for me to get an education.

Partly I was just unhappy. But part of it was that, freshman year, I started getting picked on. In class, one kid would always ask me a question about what the teacher had just said.

I'd answer back, "I don't know."

Then right away he'd start saying, "Damn, you don't know nothing, you're so dumb."

Things like that would happen a lot. Whatever people said would get to me.

From Dropout to Achiever

For the most part, I thought my school was safe. It had a reputation for being one of the better schools. But in the middle of my freshman year I got a taste of how bad things were going to get.

Before Christmas vacation, I'd had an argument with a kid on the bus. Afterward, I didn't think that much about it. But when we returned from break, he attacked me from behind and pummeled me while I was on the ground.

I missed two weeks of school because of the bruises inflicted on my face.

After it happened, my mom and I went to the police station and filed a report, but he didn't get arrested. I told the dean of my high school and showed him who did it to me. But he didn't get suspended.

Sometimes a bunch of kids would surround one kid and ask him, "Yo, you got some money?"

A couple days after I returned to school, I saw him again on the bus and he was laughing and bragging about beating me up.

After that, I would sit in class and think about what happened a lot. Since some other kids in the school were still talking about the fight, I couldn't get it off my mind. I felt humiliated, and I felt an anger that I couldn't let go of. It's not that I didn't want to learn. I just couldn't get my mind to concentrate.

I've had trouble concentrating in school before. I've been left back because I've had difficulties learning. But being in my high school didn't help.

In my sophomore year, some kids began wearing beads and joining gangs or just forming into groups. Every once in a while I would see one of my friends hanging outside near the school and he'd act like he wanted to ignore me. I figured they didn't want to talk to anyone who was not as tough as they were.

Inside the school, fistfights would sometimes break out. Outside, gangs and smaller groups would walk around looking for someone to rob, intimidate, or beat up. They would look for anyone who seemed weak and they would hurt them for fun.

Then they would laugh as they walked away, bragging about what they'd done.

Sometimes a bunch of kids would surround one kid and ask him, "Yo, you got some money?" and he would give them what he had.

One time I was sitting in the bus and across the highway I saw at least 15 guys attacking this one Russian kid. I didn't see the whole thing because the bus was already moving. But as I sat there I imagined how scared that kid must have been. He probably knew what they were going to do to him but didn't know how to stop them.

Every time I was outside the school I had to make sure I didn't stare at anyone or else he might take it as a challenge. And when I left school I had to make sure that nobody was following me.

This one kid at my school who I knew was pressured to rob other kids. Earlier in high school he hadn't been a troublemaker —he was more of a joker. We'd see each other in resource room, where we went to get help on our weak subjects. He would make jokes about the resource teacher and I would crack up. Then I would make a comment about her and we'd keep cracking up laughing.

But in our sophomore year, some kids from his neighborhood were always trying to convince him to rob somebody after school. Even though I knew he wasn't the type, twice I saw him hustle some guys for change. He didn't threaten anyone, and it seemed like he didn't really want to do it. I think he just couldn't say no, especially to his friends.

I think the reason people in my school were acting this way was because they wanted respect. They were probably angry because they didn't get respect anywhere else, like in their homes or in their neighborhoods. They probably wanted to show people they were not to be messed with.

But I felt it was wrong to hurt other people for no reason. When I saw kids getting beat up, I sympathized with them because I knew how they felt when they went home, bruised and humiliated. The more threatened I felt outside my school, the more alone I felt.

> **When I saw kids getting beat up, I sympathized with them because I knew how they felt when they went home.**

By the end of my junior year, the safety around the school did improve.

I guess most of the really violent students were either placed in another school, kicked out or they just dropped out. We had gone through a couple of principals and the school was getting tougher on suspending people as soon as they got into a fight.

Now when I go to school I see a lot more police outside a lot more of the time. Things seem safer.

Right now I have an internship, so I don't attend school on a regular basis. And I'm glad that in January I'll be graduating. I'm tired of high school and the people in it.

My mother always used to tell me that you can't get a decent job without a high school diploma. She explained how hard it was for her because she dropped out her freshman year. So I never really thought of dropping out and I'm glad I didn't.

Next year I plan to get a full-time or part-time job and I want to go to college. Eventually I'd like to work in a music studio. Still, when I think of the future, I'm concerned about getting a good job to support myself.

Sometimes I think it would have been better if I had been more aggressive, and just knocked someone after he said one word to me. But then I realize that wouldn't have solved anything.

I may have thought I was weak compared to the tough guys, but there was one good thing about being quiet and a loner. I didn't feel pressured to do things I knew were wrong. I didn't have to prove anything to anyone, like my friend from the neighborhood who started robbing.

In some ways I had to be strong in order to not follow what everyone else was doing.

Omar was 19 when he wrote this story.
He later worked in the printing industry.

Sticking With Your 'Own Kind'

By Cassandra Thadal

Here's a scene from a typical day in my high school classroom: students from various countries, such as Mexico, Poland, Bangladesh, Yemen, and the Dominican Republic, are talking and laughing as they work together and help each other.

The teacher yells, "Why am I hearing you talking? Shouldn't you be working?"

"We work and talk at the same time," we answer.

When the clock marks lunchtime, we run eagerly out of our classroom and head for the cafeteria. But by the time we reach our destination, the kids who mixed happily in the classroom have left that spirit of unity behind.

At most of the tables in the cafeteria, you see faces of the same color. The students enjoy this time with their own folks. The kids say they do this because it's just more comfortable. So whoever

Sticking With Your 'Own Kind'

arrives in the cafeteria first gets her food and spots some seats, then saves a place for others of her same race or ethnic group.

After lunch, they leave together and spend the rest of the period in the hallways, or outside if it's not cold. A group of Polish kids settles on the floor near the main office, chatting and gossiping. Sometimes other Polish kids play checkers or dice nearby.

Some of the Dominicans sit in the hallway a few feet from the Polish kids. Most of the time they talk loudly and sing in Spanish or dance. A little further along some kids from Ecuador or Peru hang out. The Bengalis gather in one classroom, listening to Bengali music.

At most of the tables in the cafeteria, you see faces of the same color.

The Haitian girls—the group I am part of—hang out next to our counselor's office, while the Haitian boys assemble on the stairs.

The students are allowed to roam around freely like this because my school is very small and generally there's harmony. People may have their personal disagreements, but groups rarely fight. That doesn't mean that everybody's friends, though—they aren't.

Of course, some teens do befriend people from different races. One Polish girl often hangs with a Philippina girl, and there are two black guys, one from France, the other from Africa, who are friends with a kid from Mexico.

I am also someone who doesn't stick only to my own race—although this wasn't always the case. When I first arrived here I had never spent any time with white people.

I lived in Haiti until I was 14. When I saw white people in Haiti, I hated them because I knew that whites had enslaved and mistreated blacks. I didn't know any whites who considered blacks equal.

Also, some Haitians said, "Oh, the whites are so smart!"

whenever they saw great things like computers or cars, as if no black person could invent things. I hated that.

When I moved to the U.S., I began to experience being around people of other races. I sat in a classroom and saw all different kinds of people. I wanted to talk to them—except the whites. My friends were Chinese, Honduran, and Haitian.

But when I saw the white kids, I said to myself, "I am not going to talk to these people." I assumed they were saying the same thing because I'm black. But gradually my attitude changed.

I realized I had become a different person by not mixing with other students.

The white kids at school treated me nicely, and I saw that many blacks were doing great at my school. It seemed like in the U.S., whether you're black or white, you can do great things. In class I learned that we all had things in common and I began to feel comfortable. My friends and I often discussed racism. We thought that teenagers should mix. Our culture and skin color differed but we ignored our differences in the classroom and got along very well.

So it surprised me that when I returned to school last fall, I stopped mingling with other races and stayed with two Haitian girls. It didn't happen that way because I was being a racist, or at least I didn't think so.

It was because my Honduran friend, Daysa, was not yet back from vacation, and most of my old Chinese friends were in other classes. So every day during lunch, I started sitting with the Haitian girls.

After Daysa came back, I still spent most of my time with the Haitians. Daysa spoke with her friends in Spanish and I spoke Haitian Creole with my friends. I didn't see any problem with this until one day I got to the lunchroom before my two Haitian friends.

A friend of mine from the Dominican Republic asked me to sit with her, so I did. When my Haitian friends came, they looked

Sticking With Your 'Own Kind'

at me strangely, but I didn't react and just said, "Hi." Then I ate my lunch and talked to the Dominican girl.

Later, when my Haitian friends were leaving, they passed and said, "Oh, yeah, Cassandra, you're buying the Spanish face." ("Buying someone's face" is a Haitian expression. It means that you ignore your own race and stay with another one because you think that the other race is superior, even if that race is disrespectful to you.)

I laughed and said, "What do you mean I'm buying the Spanish face? Sitting with someone Spanish has nothing to do with that." Later I talked with one of my friends and told her that what they said wasn't fair and didn't make me happy.

"OK, girl," she said, and that was it. We were again at peace.

I didn't take these things too seriously. They sounded more like jokes to me. But soon I realized they were not jokes. Later in the year, I became friends with a Russian girl named Natasha. We were in the same group in class and she was very nice to me. We always talked to each other in class and she often called me on the telephone, but we never sat together at lunch.

One day my Haitian friends were sitting at our table while I was still standing in line. After I got my meal I saw Natasha and she called to me.

"Come sit with me!"

"Oh...I'm sorry. I have to sit with the Haitians or else they would say that I'm buying your face. You know..."

"What?" Natasha said, confused. I explained the expression and she said, "OK, I'll see you later."

I left her by herself and went to my other friends. Because I didn't want my Haitian friends to tease me, I stopped hanging out with people of other races.

Sometimes in the morning I still walked around with one of the Chinese guys who had been my friend since 9th grade. My friends from Haiti never said anything about that, but another Haitian girl told me, "Cassandra, you love the Chinese too much.

47

From Dropout to Achiever

You're buying their faces."

I laughed and told her she was wrong. Still, I kept my friendship with kids from other races inside the classroom, because I hated what my Haitian friends said whenever I hung out with them at lunch.

The Haitian students mean a lot to me and I always try to get along with them because they're my people. I never told them how much I was bothered by what they said. Then I started to write this story, and I began to think about how we were all acting.

I realized I had become a different person by not mixing with other students when I wanted to. And when I realized that, I decided to change back to who I really am.

Now, in the cafeteria, I sit with Natasha, my Russian friend, along with my Honduran friend, Daysa.

I had stopped mixing with other kids because I was scared of what my friends would think and say. It's good to stay with "your people" sometimes. But, at the same time, if you only stay with your people, you're missing out on a lot of opportunities to make new friends and have new experiences.

We need to break down the walls of language, culture, and skin color if we want racism to stop. We share many common things, but the only way we can find out what they are is if we mix.

Cassandra was 15 when she wrote this story.
She went on to graduate from high school and college.

Getting Guys Off My Back

By Artiqua Steed

My freshman year in high school was a difficult one, mostly because of my ex-boyfriend. Marcus would touch me in the hallways or make disgusting comments having to do with sex. Once during summer school he caught me in the staircase alone and tried to kiss me.

I hated him. Having to see his face every day was so unnerving. I felt uncomfortable in school because of him.

Guys had said and done things like that to me on the streets, but I never expected to have to deal with that kind of behavior in my own school. I thought I was safe there. In fact, at the school's orientation, my parents and I were assured that it was a safe place. So why wasn't I safe from Marcus's obnoxious behavior?

I was angry but I did nothing about it. I couldn't go and tell on him because then I would be known as the school rat. I just gave Marcus dirty looks, hoping he would leave me alone.

What made it worse was that Marcus's friends started bothering me. After that, I couldn't even walk down the corridor without someone saying something totally perverted to me. One guy even came up to me and asked me if he could touch me. Did he actually believe that I would let him? I wanted to slap him for disrespecting me, but I didn't. He probably would have hit me back.

"Is it a curse?" I wondered. "Why is this happening to me? Why are guys so disgustingly stupid?"

I was being sexually harassed, but it took me a while to realize it, maybe because no one ever talks about it in school. Sure, they have sex education classes and even some parenting classes, but nothing is said about sexual harassment.

Not long after that, my friend Stephanie told me that when she was in junior high school, the guys used to harass her nonstop. Boys would grab her. One guy went as far as trapping her in the school bathroom where he tried to kiss her. Hearing her story made me understand what a serious problem sexual harassment is. I became determined not to let any guy harass me and get away with it ever again.

Marcus would touch me in the hallways or make disgusting comments having to do with sex.

A couple of months ago, I was standing in the hall at school with my friend Derek. While I was talking to him, another guy, Jason, walked by me and touched my butt. Now, I've known Jason for two years and he was cool with me.

I couldn't believe what he had done. At first I was dumbfounded and couldn't say a word. Then I started yelling at him. He walked away laughing.

Derek was trying to calm me down. Then Jason came back towards me. I jumped at him and tried to slap him. I only touched a small part of his face because he had grabbed my arms when he saw what I was going to do.

I yelled, "Let me go!" and went to hit him again. Then Jason grabbed me and put me up against the wall. He didn't do it hard, it was just enough to pin me to the wall. When he let me go I was very, very upset. I could feel the heat rising off my face.

Derek didn't do anything while this was going on. I was mad at him for that. He told me that I was overreacting. I wanted to hit him too. But what would you expect from a guy? I don't think most guys understand how it feels to be sexually harassed.

I know that the way I handled it was not the best way. But I have to admit that it did make me feel better to hit Jason. I got my anger out.

I had to go back to class after that. Two minutes after I sat down, Jason walked in. When class was over I walked up to him and said, "You're in trouble." (Actually I said something else, but I can't write those words down.) Then I walked out of class.

Jason stormed out after me. He was like, "Why are you going to tell? Can't we just squash this? You did slap me." So I said to him, "Yes, I did slap you but not like I wanted to. And I slapped you because you touched me." Then he said something so stupid. He said, "Whatever you do, don't ever talk to me again. Just act like you don't know me!"

That made me even madder than I already was. Why would I want to talk to him after what he did to me? I started yelling at him all over again. One of the teachers heard and came out to ask me what happened.

After I told her, she told the co-director of my school. The next day a conference was held and I got to tell my story to the co-director.

They called Jason in and he denied everything that happened. Even so, the co-director believed me. Not because I'm a girl but because this boy was not a good liar. He could not get his story straight even if he had taped it on his forehead.

First he said that he didn't even know me. Then he said that

From Dropout to Achiever

I just walked up to him and slapped him. The co-director asked him why I would slap him if I didn't know him. So then Jason said that we always play around in the hall like that. That made me want to hit him again, just for lying. But I controlled myself.

The next day the co-director came and commended me for speaking up about what happened and for not letting Jason get away with what he did. I don't know what happened to Jason because I was sent out of the room after I told my side of the story.

All I know is that I always see Jason in the halls and he is still in one of my classes. He has never bothered me again but he acts as if nothing has happened. He even asked me for a dollar the other day. I just looked at him like he was crazy.

I feel good about the fact that I didn't let Jason get away with harassing me. I'm also glad that my voice was heard. If something like that ever happens to me again I will do the same thing I did in this case (except I won't hit the person).

> **I was being sexually harassed, but it took me a while to realize it because no one ever talks about it in school.**

But I also think more should be done about sexual harassment in school. School shouldn't be a place where you feel uncomfortable. It should be a positive learning environment.

I think that schools should educate their students about what to do in these situations so they won't be scared to come forward. The schools should let students know that if they're harassed, they'll have people on their side, supporting them. That way more and more people will be encouraged to fight against sexual harassment in the schools. And the harassers will realize that they won't get away with it.

Artiqua wrote this story when she was 16. She went on to graduate from high school and study business administration.

Black Girl, White School

By Angelina Darrisaw

In 7th grade I was the only black girl in my class, and it was strange. I knew my new school was going to be predominantly white, but I didn't realize I'd be the only black person in my grade for two years.

I'm from a black neighborhood and even though I knew of having a few white relatives, until 7th grade I had little interaction with white people.

Through 6th grade, I went to an all-black public school where I got joked on for being light skinned and having long wavy hair. My old classmates had called me white girl, but at my new school it was instantly clear that I was a black girl—surrounded by actual white girls.

I ended up at my school though a program that places gifted children, mostly of color, into private schools. My mom put me

From Dropout to Achiever

through the 14-month program because she saw it as an educational opportunity.

I applied and got accepted to the school I attend now. My mom chose it because it was small, with only about 400 students from nursery to 12th grade. We also felt, after our visits, that it was less snooty than others and that its Catholic background gave it a warm feel.

I was shy at first. But my classmates were so friendly it was easy for me to open up. They asked about my old school, my family, the shows I liked, and my hobbies. Still, sometimes I felt they were asking those questions out of duty, not out of interest.

Even though my classmates were generally friendly, they kept me aware that I was the only black girl. Sometimes it was like I represented the entire black race. Whenever anyone mentioned someone black or something about being black, my class would look at me.

Classmates asked me, "What do black people like to be called, African-American or black?" I told them, "I can only speak for myself."

I was the only black girl in my class, but there were a few other black students in the school. The school made two of them, a senior and a junior, talk to me weekly, claiming it was because I was new. But none of the other new girls met with two older students. It was just me. Meeting with those girls helped because we shared experiences and they dropped knowledge, but it only added to my feeling of being separate and different.

My classmates seemed to assume that I and other black girls lived in some TV-type ghetto where everyone was a gang member and I had to dodge bullets to get home. My neighborhood is actually quiet most of the time and people keep to themselves.

Some comments were so ignorant I had to laugh about it later, though I still found them offensive. I was amazed my schoolmates could be that sheltered. A lot of people also assumed that all the minority kids were on financial aid when that wasn't the case.

It was the more general statements from classmates about poor people and blacks that killed me though, like "most people on welfare are black," which isn't true. It was clear we had different realities. My life was something they could only hear about and wouldn't dream of living.

And it was weird because I thought I was better off than a lot of kids. But because I didn't have a maid and designer clothes, I was poor by their standards.

Our different backgrounds led us to different political opinions, too. Most of the girls were pro-Republican and pro-rich. At my old school, it was the opposite. So I was shocked to discover that people could favor programs and government officials who I thought cared little for most of the city's residents.

Until 7th grade, I had little interaction with white people.

I got into heated debates with some of my classmates about the problems with our capitalist system, or why affirmative action could be justified or how slavery was no fault of Africans. It was frustrating, not just coming up against opinions I thought were wrong, but that I was now the only one with my opinions. I had to constantly defend my perspective.

Our different upbringings made it hard to relate on some issues, but girls are girls. We liked boys, food, music, and going out. So sometimes we could connect on that level.

But then differences still remained. I preferred black boys, they preferred white boys. They'd meet guys at the joint school dances with private all-girl and all-boy schools. I could count on one hand how many black guys went there, so I'd meet guys through my old school, my neighborhood, or my church.

We also had different ideas of what was fun. A lot of them smoked, drank, or shopped for fun. My friends and I danced and went to movies for our fun.

From Dropout to Achiever

Maybe it's because of these differences that my classmates didn't invite me to their parties and dances. One of them told me at the end of 7th grade, when I asked her why I didn't get invited to her party, that they didn't invite me because they felt I would be uninterested.

I wasn't sure what she meant by that, but I think if I'd been invited, I'd have gone without hesitation. I wanted to have friends in a new school like everybody else. It hurt to be left out.

Not having any good friends at school and always feeling alone made me miserable. I felt like I was in kindergarten all over again, being called white girl and excluded from playing double-dutch. But now I was excluded because I was black.

By the end of the year I'd had enough. I really wanted to change schools and sometimes came home in tears because I hated my school so much.

"Mommy, I can't take it anymore," I screamed at home one day. "Come on! Let me go to another school, puhleeeeeeze!"

Mom wasn't hearing that. "Sweetie, I know it can get tough, but what do you think the real world is going to be like? No matter where you go, there's going to be problems and I don't want you changing schools. End of story."

I thought she was just making excuses, and that she didn't want me to change schools because the admission process had been so hard. But down deep, I knew she was right.

So I stuck it out. The following year, when we had elections for grade representatives, to my surprise, I was nominated. I guess my classmates liked the way I spoke my mind and had an opinion on everything, because I was elected. That made me feel less alienated and more liked.

But I still wasn't cool enough for anyone in my class to invite me to hang. I had to take the initiative and invite them downtown or to a movie. Sometimes they joined me, but I felt like a friendship shouldn't be so one-sided.

So I was happy to connect with the few other black students

in the grades above me. Many of us went home from school the same way and had similar interests and upbringings. So we made an effort to call each other and really be friends—in school and out.

We came from a variety of backgrounds and classes, but our cultural similarities—and our experience of feeling excluded—brought us together. At lunch, we often sat at the same table in the teahouse (my school's version of a cafeteria) every day.

It's not like we had a sign that said "No Whites Allowed!" But some people at school thought we were excluding others. The administration told us to break it up.

It became a whole big drama questioning why the black kids were always together, but we saw it as white people always sitting together. We, who connected after being excluded, were told that we were excluding people. We were just friends who liked being with each other and were rarely invited to sit with white schoolmates, so why couldn't we be together?

My classmates assumed that I lived in the ghetto and had to dodge bullets to get home.

The drama continued into my freshman year, with assemblies about how people felt about the issue and student-teacher groups organized to discuss it.

Many students, black and white, didn't think it was such a big deal. We thought the teachers were overdoing it. We made more of an effort to mix with the white students, but most of the time, we still sat together.

If I could do prep school over again, I probably wouldn't. But as I'm getting older, I see that I have to make the best of it, or at least try to. Knowing hundreds of other kids are going through the same thing makes it easier because there's always someone to talk to.

And while going to an elite private school is often a strain socially, academically I'm happy. I've taken fantastic classes in literature and modern world history and participated in a model congress.

This September marks my fourth year there. And soon, I'm going to be the junior or senior who's asked to talk to the shy, new black 7th grader.

I guess I'll just say, "Hey, I'm always here to talk. It gets hard sometimes, but being here, you get opportunities that will be really important in the long run. Remember, you're in school to learn. And you gotta make yourself happy."

Angelina was 15 when she wrote this story. After completing high school she earned a bachelor's degree from Davidson College and a master's degree in management from Wake Forest, and then she went to work for a major television network.

Dropout Blues

By Diana Moreno

My life as a drop out. Where do I begin?

I guess you could say that I came to a fork in the road and chose to follow the wrong path to reach my goal—you know, a short cut. I thought I had found an easy way out from the hard work I dreaded. But I learned there is no such thing as a short cut, an easy way out—you have to work hard in order to make it.

I guess that's why I'm here now telling you what dropping out of school was like for me, and why I decided to return.

I'm in school now because I've decided that I want to have that diploma to wave around like a gold medal. I have set myself up with a goal to graduate high school—and that's what I'm going to do.

It isn't always easy, and I still think about dropping out. Sometimes I feel like I always have that white surrender flag flapping in the air and I feel like a loser and that I'm not going to make it.

But then I think of my family, the ones who always say, "I told you so," and I snap and realize I can't do that to myself. Then I try to crawl out of that big black gaping hole that I have dug for myself.

So let me get back to the story and tell you a little about my school mess-up and myself.

First off, before you read this and think, "Hell, she's one of those girls who probably never made it past junior high school without the help of the soft teachers," I just have to prove you wrong.

Growing up, I was basically your average bookworm, or what my peers used to call me—a NERD. I always had my hand up in class. If I passed a test, I didn't mind showing it off. Kids called me a geek because I didn't just turn in my homework, I did extra credit, too.

I liked school, and the first time I dropped out, at the start of my freshman year, it was more of an accident. I had just moved to live with my mom, but I was supposed to be attending a school far away in another neighborhood, and the travel time was hectic. So I tried to transfer out.

My mom had all the papers, but I was told that it was too late to transfer and I would have to wait for the February term to begin.

At the time, my mom, well, she was in another world. She had her own problems to deal with. And with no one making sure I got my act together, I just let everything slide. In fact, I wound up staying out of school for the whole year. I kind of enjoyed myself in the beginning. But the fun came to a halt when the warm days began to fade.

I found myself constantly alone—everyone was moving on and I was just sitting still while the action passed me by.

I would be home doing nothing, gaining weight, lying in bed

watching TV or reading, while my friends were in school, and I would hope for 3 o'clock to hurry up and come so that I could go and chill.

What's amazing is that after a few weeks I found myself craving school and wanting to make my brain bigger. I would actually go and do my friend's brother's homework.

I used to get all hyped when he told me he got an A or B plus on an assignment I did for him. At first, I didn't mind too much that he was getting credit for my work because I had a crush on him. But later I decided that he'd better do his own work, and I went back to being bored.

It was easy to cut. All my friends were cutting, too, and so I was pulled in.

There wasn't much I could do during the day. I was scared to go outside because I was underage and didn't want the cops to pick me up and put my mom in problems. Plus, it was starting to get cold—always looking like it was going to rain.

But it bothered me knowing that my friends were in school while I was home slowly deteriorating. I found myself reading books with words I'd never heard of and looking up the meanings, so I'd understand and develop my vocabulary.

I liked to find ways to use my new-found knowledge in my sentences and have people comment, "Hey, you're a smart kid." But I dreaded what came next: "Then why aren't you in school?" Someone always found a way to bust my bubble. I began to feel that my future had no real meaning unless I was in school, and I wanted to return.

But the person who really got me back in school was my uncle. He literally dragged me from school to school trying to get me in. We went to three schools in the same day—and we were walking. I had blisters on my feet by the time I got home.

"You're going to school whether you like it or not," he raved. "You've wasted enough time and that's final!" The next day I was

From Dropout to Achiever

enrolled.

When I returned, I already had it in my mind that I was going to pass all of my classes and be on the honor roll and return to the kind of student I used to be. But that only lasted one quarter of the semester. I was so used to not being in school that it was hard for me to get used to the class rules and get focused.

I started out my days saying that I was going to succeed—but I found I was behind more than I had expected.

I constantly felt like I was under water and needed some air to breathe. "How am I going to catch up?" I wondered. What made it harder was that I was also trying to prove myself to people in my family.

See, in my family, there aren't many graduates. My mom never made it past 9th grade and she repeated it three times. My uncle Luis made it to college but never completed his course of study. Still, he, my mom, and my grandma instill in me the desire for an education.

I would daydream about my senior prom and graduation, with my whole family there clapping, cheering, and crying.

But other people in my family, like my aunt Lucy, fill me with doubt. She tells me I'm too high up on my horse and soon I'm going to fall off, and sometimes that negative talk makes it easier for me to fall.

I always said I wasn't going to be like my family, I was going to make it, but when I found school hard and began to mess up, I found myself thinking, "Oh my God, maybe I am nothing and am destined to be nothing," and that scared me.

Besides, it was easy to cut. All my friends were cutting, too. It would be "Come on, Diana—let's go chill. Come on, after today you could stop but just for today let's go do something. Come on, it's only the beginning of the term—these first few days of classes don't really matter, you could make it up later," and so I was pulled in.

And at my school, anyone wanting to leave the building

could just walk right on out past security. They don't care what happens to us once we go out those doors, and actually, I don't blame them—we make our choices for ourselves. If we want to learn, we go to school—if we don't, we become no shows. Which is what I became.

By January I found myself cutting more and more by myself. After a while I would only show up for two or three periods and then I would leave. Usually I would cut at least one full day of classes each week. Instead, I would just hang around, explore the stores, and chill at Mickey D's when it got chilly.

All that time, I didn't really see past the next day or week or month, and I assumed I had all the time in the world to correct my mistakes. The only time I thought about the future was when I was daydreaming. I would daydream about my senior prom and my graduation, with my whole family there clapping and cheering, some crying that I actually made it.

But sometimes I'd blink and I'd be back to the present and it was "Oh WOW! I have a lot to accomplish and so little time to do it." And if you're like me, this is usually the time where you get stuck and shake your head like a wet dog shakes his body and say to yourself, "What am I going to do?"

But after I pulled my hair out a little, I would get laid back and tell myself, "Oh, well, no one's perfect." I would convince myself that my family couldn't be mad at me because they didn't make it anywhere themselves.

At the end of the year when I got my final report card, I realized I only had seven credits for the whole year. I laughed at this, but I also decided again that next year I would do better. But I didn't. By November, I was already messing up.

I would go to school feeling that this time I was going to make it, then things would appear harder than they really were. I would get frustrated and search for an escape.

In February I decided to enroll in a class to get my GED, in order to not have to go through the stressing ordeal of high school. But I was bored, and after about three weeks I dropped that, too.

I worked full-time at a store, and when I wasn't at work I was lying down watching TV. Sometimes I watched talk shows from 11 a.m. until 5 p.m. I was very lazy, tired all the time. I gained a lot of weight and felt worse and worse about myself.

Then I got even more depressed, quit my job, and was stressed most of the day. I was your average couch potato.

During the spring and through the summer, all I remember thinking was "Damn, now I have no job, no money and no school to keep me busy." I was of age to work, but I couldn't find a job.

But in May I heard about City-As-School and I decided to apply. It's an alternative high school and you work in the business world for your school credits.

Now that I'm in school, for the most part I enjoy it. Sometimes I get a little hectic and those old feelings come back to haunt me. Like today, I went to school to discuss when I'll be graduating.

I looked at my transcript and I needed so many credits. I thought, "I'm never going to make it." But you know what? This time I'm going to try to take things at my own steady pace.

I still don't have my act completely together. I'm still struggling. I still have doubts.

When I mess up, it's kind of like a tornado—it swirls and swirls and it doesn't end until it's done with all of its destruction. Then I pick up the pieces and start over, because the worst has already happened. All that's left is the endless effort to fix and correct.

Still, I get sad and mad at myself because this is not what I want to be doing with myself.

I guess I'm beginning to think of my life like that old folktale, "The Turtle and the Rabbit." The rabbit was always looking for the shortcuts, sure he was going to win the race. The turtle took his time.

The rabbit relaxed. He napped. But soon he awoke and realized the turtle was inches from winning the race. The rabbit became hectic and tried to rush, but the turtle reached the finish line first, and the rabbit lost.

I was that silly rabbit—but slowly I'm becoming that turtle. I will make it and reach my finish line. I won't give up. I'm going to graduate no matter what. I'm going to stay in school and not only prove myself to my family, but prove myself to myself.

Diana was 18 when she wrote this story.
After high school she joined Americorps.

When Great Isn't Good Enough

By Janill Briones

It was a tiring day at school and I was glad to be going home. The last period I'd gotten my chemistry test back and was happy to see that I got a 91.

As I opened the door, I found my mom where I usually find her, over the sink preparing dinner and washing the dishes.

"Hi, dear. How was your day?" she said, in Spanish.

"It was fine. I got my test back for chemistry. Look, I got a 91."

"Let me see it," she said, drying her hands on the dishtowel and taking the test paper. "Just a 91."

"Mom, that's really good compared to what everybody else got."

"Mm-hmm, and what did your friend get?"

"Oh, I think she got a 95 or something."

"I guess she studied more than you did, didn't she?" she said, handing me back the test.

I stomped out of the kitchen. It was typical of her to say that. I was so mad.

She makes me feel like I'm not good enough. I sometimes ask myself, "Why does she have to be like that?" The only answer I can think of is that maybe she pushes me hard to do well in school because she never got the education she wanted.

Both my parents were born in Ecuador. Around their way there were no schools after 3rd grade. So after 3rd grade my dad stopped studying and started to help his parents by selling things like eggs.

My mom was able to get further. She was sent away to school until the 6th grade. Then when she was 16, she studied with the nuns for four years, learning mostly about religion and nursing. She was on her way to becoming a nun until she decided to get married and have children.

Even though neither of them made it through high school, my parents are very smart. Ever since they came here about 18 years ago, they've been able to support my younger brother Ronald and me, and I'm proud of them.

Dad works at a racetrack cleaning floors. I think he'd have loved to do something else, but he couldn't get far with the education he had. He has a positive attitude, though, and says that at least he's able to have food on the table for us every night.

Dad works at a racetrack cleaning floors. He couldn't get far with the education he had.

Mom used to work in a factory, but now she's dedicated to staying home and taking care of Ronald and me and the house. I think she's proud of being a housewife. Still, Mom and Dad want a much better life for me.

Their focus on education started early. Before I began kin-

From Dropout to Achiever

dergarten, Mom showed me basic addition and subtraction. I remember her sitting on the couch while I knelt on the floor next to her, paying close attention to what she was telling me. (She couldn't really teach me reading because she spoke Spanish and didn't know how to read or write much in English.)

When I hit kindergarten, I was the best student in the class in math. And it was like that from then on. I enjoyed getting good grades, but I also liked making my mom proud of me. She always congratulated me on my grades.

But in junior high, things began to get tougher. My grades went down, not dramatically, but enough to make my mom disappointed. Instead of the usual 100s and 95s, I was getting some 90s and 85s. Even a drop of a point on my report card upset her.

Whenever I brought home an imperfect test, she'd go into one of her speeches. "You see, next time try harder and you will succeed," or, "You should have studied more, then maybe you would have gotten a 100." She even started to use reverse psychology on me. She'd say I couldn't do things so I'd feel bad and try harder to prove to her that I could do it.

By 7th grade, I decided to show her only my best grades. Even now, I seldom tell her when I'm having a test.

When I do bring home an excellent grade, like a 100, she sounds like she doesn't care. She says stuff like "Good," and "Great," but she doesn't congratulate me like she does with Ronald, who's a year younger than me.

He doesn't do as well in school as I do—his grades are usually in the high 70s and 80s—but she doesn't get on his case as much as she gets on mine.

When I was 15, I saw my mom congratulate Ron for a good grade. I asked her, "Why is it that when I get a good grade you just ignore it and say, 'OK,' but when Ronald gets a good grade, it's a party?"

"That's not true," she said. "I'm always happy when you give me a good grade."

"Well, you sure don't show it. You always say, 'Mm-hmm,' or 'That's nice.' "

"That's because I know you have the potential to do it. That's why you always have to put your batteries on, so that you can reach the top, and nobody will be able to stop you," she said, raising her right hand in a fist and slamming it back down against her left palm.

It's nice to know that she's behind me, but it's too much pressure to feel like I have to be perfect. When I wasn't valedictorian for elementary or junior high school, Mom was upset because it meant that I wasn't the best. I thought it was kind of silly to care about that. I mean, I wasn't valedictorian, but I certainly had a high ranking.

I think Mom might be afraid that if I'm not the best, I might turn into one of those girls she watches out the window, walking in their slippers and ragged clothes, not really caring about their appearance, the ones who've dropped out of school and hang out with boys all the time.

Whenever I brought home an imperfect test, Mom would go into one of her speeches.

She knows from experience that it's hard to go through life without an education, but I find it annoying to hear the same thing over and over again.

I've never given her any reason to worry that I'd drop out of school to hang out all the time. She knows me better than that, but she sure doesn't act like it.

I blow up sometimes when I get too much from her, like when she says I'm "malcriada," which means someone who misbehaves. When she's so critical, it makes me feel almost as if she wants me to be somebody else, somebody better. That hurts me.

"I do study! The tests are hard. So what if I miss a few questions!"

"That's not the point," she says. "You should study every day so that you can get a better score. One day when you're older and

From Dropout to Achiever

have your own place to live and a job, you're going to come back and say, 'Thank you, Mom, for all you've done.' You just watch."

It's irritating, but in a way, I think she's right. As much as my mom's constant nagging about my schoolwork drives me crazy, I don't think I'd be as careful with my schoolwork without it. I also might not care as much about my education, though you won't catch me telling her that.

But I do take my work and my grades seriously—for me, not for Mom. I know perfectly well that it's going to help me in life, not her. That's why I chose to go a competitive school, Science Skills Center HS, and why last quarter I received 90s and above in all my classes except for an 85 in global history.

I wish my mom would see how much I try and would be more encouraging. My father supports me more. Sometimes when he's around, he backs me up when my mom starts bugging me about my grades. It feels good to have a fan.

I know the support is there. Mom drops hints to me about how much doctors make, even though I've told her I want to be a journalist. But when people ask her what my goals are, she tells them proudly that I want to be a journalist.

I know my mom loves me and is proud of me. I'd just feel a whole lot better if she'd show me that she's my fan, too.

Janill graduated high school and went on to college, where she majored in psychology, specializing in animal behavior. She was 16 when she wrote this story.

They Called Me a 'Crack Baby'

By Antwaun Garcia

I don't know if I was born with drugs in my body or not. But my moms used drugs while she was pregnant with me. So it wasn't long before kids at school were calling me a "crack baby."

It started in 4th grade. My teacher asked me to read from a Dr. Seuss book. I struggled with the first word. Maybe it's because I actually was born with crack in my system. Or maybe it's just because my home was chaotic and my parents never sat me down and read me stories or taught me the ABC's.

At the time, I lived across from one of the most notorious crack houses in my neighborhood. My pops was a well-known pimp, and he and all my uncles hustled for a living. The fact that my home was filled with chaos showed, and not just because I couldn't read. I went to school every day looking like a bum, and my clothes smelled like cat piss.

From Dropout to Achiever

As I struggled trying to read, the other kids began to giggle. Then this one kid, who lived near me and knew about my living conditions said, "He can't read because he's a crack baby." Everyone turned to stare at me.

I had never heard the expression "crack baby," so I sat there looking plumb dumb, trying to figure it out. I thought, "What, babies who sniff crack?" I knew I didn't do things like that.

The other kids were looking at me like I had a disease and the teacher was having a hard time keeping them quiet. Eventually she gave up and just apologized to me. I kept wondering, "Is there something wrong with me?"

> **I went to school every day looking like a bum and my clothes smelled like cat piss.**

The next day no one wanted to sit next to me during lunch, and they pointed fingers at me. I couldn't really eat. How can you when you have half of the school cafeteria looking at you? I was embarrassed and ashamed of myself and where I lived.

From that day on, just about all the kids in 4th grade began calling me "slow," "dirty," and "crack baby." I started to believe those things about myself and I constantly imagined what the kids were saying to each other about me. I felt stupid and worthless.

So I stopped going to class. Soon the only time I came to school was to get free lunch and go to the gym, but even that I didn't do too often. I started staying out on the street or at my man's crib helping him cut cocaine.

Then I moved to a new neighborhood when I was 10. That's when I went into foster care and moved in with my aunt. I missed my family and friends in the old neighborhood, but in some ways I was really relieved to move and change schools. No one knew about my home life, and my aunt gave me good clothes and made sure I was clean.

My first day of class, the teacher asked me to read. I still didn't know how, so I hesitated, remembering what happened to me before. I asked the teacher to ask someone else to read and she did. That was a relief, but I knew I couldn't keep dodging teachers forever. I'd need to learn how to read and write. To do it, I had to let go of the label "crack baby." I had to believe I could learn.

And basically, with my aunt and teachers' help, I did learn to read and write at age 10. It took a lot of time and work. Sometimes I thought it was too hard. Some nights I cried myself to sleep because I missed my family and it was too hard to catch up with the other kids in my class.

But I didn't quit. And it wasn't long before I was in the top classes in the school. Now, 10 years later, that kid who was called a crack baby is in college about to get his Associates degree. I am not done yet. I have a lot more things to accomplish in my life, and I am not letting no one or no label hold me back from achieving anything.

Sometimes I go back to my old neighborhood and see some of the kids from that class where I got labeled a crack baby. Though a lot of them are in trouble now, and a lot haven't accomplished anywhere close to what I have, I still feel really angry when I see them. Those two words almost cost me an education. It's crazy how powerful two words can be.

Antwaun was 20 when he wrote this story. He attended college and then got a job a major national retail company, where he worked his way up to a manager position.

The Suburbs:
A Different World

By Dean Torres

Imagine if high schools in your city were going to be closed down, and you had to travel all the way to the suburbs to go to school. Sounds bad because it's so far away, right? But guess what? It wouldn't be that bad.

For a writing assignment, I had to go to Hastings-on-Hudson, a suburb north of New York City. I interviewed students at Hastings High School and it was nice—trust me, if you had to go there, you would love it.

When I went to Hastings, I was looking forward to seeing what life is like in the suburbs. When I hit the town's shopping center, it looked like one of those towns you see on TV. The grass was nicely trimmed and there were a lot of hills. When I got to Hastings High School, it looked fancy. The classrooms were

The Suburbs: A Different World

clean, quiet, and decorated with posters. That surprised me, because in my school the classrooms are filthy. And the classes were small, about 15 or 20 students.

The school even had a student lounge with couches. And about half of the school was carpeted. That was very different from my school, which is big and has a lot of vandalism.

For my first two years of high school I went to school in Brooklyn, and it was the pits. I thought the teachers were crappy, because they didn't seem to teach you much. They also acted afraid of the students. The kids would curse the teachers out and they wouldn't say anything back to them—they'd just sit there and let the kids disrespect them. The teachers allowed it to go on every day until they finally kicked the kids out of class.

My new school is better. Some of the teachers go out of their way for the students. I had a good history teacher, and he set time aside to explain what we didn't understand. He also took time out to talk to students if they had problems.

The classrooms were clean, quiet, and decorated with posters. That surprised me, because in my school the classrooms are filthy.

But my school doesn't feel safe like Hastings. There's a lot of drugs there on the low, and students carry weapons and smoke in the bathrooms. And outside school there are gangs, drugs, and kids smoking. The gangs look for fights. Some kids don't pay it no mind, but some kids are nervous, because they're the ones who've got beef with the gang. Inside or near the school there's probably a fight once a week. That's very different from Hastings High School in the suburbs, where they said fights are rare. Hastings doesn't even have security guards!

"I don't have to look behind my back," said Meg McElroy, a Hastings senior. "We only have fights a few times a year, if there's beef."

"There's no beef in Hastings," said Tyler Morris, also a senior.

75

From Dropout to Achiever

Now, some schools in the city are probably a lot nicer than mine (friends of mine go to schools that sound cleaner and safer), and I'm sure that some suburban schools are not as clean and safe as Hastings. But it still shocked me to realize that a high school could be so different from mine.

Hastings was also different from my school because most of the kids I met there had really good grades. A lot of city kids are failing badly or dropping out.

I think the kids I met were doing so well because the students and teachers work together. The students cooperate with the teachers during class, and the teachers see that the students are willing to learn, so they show the students they care. In my school, the students are not as respectful.

One teacher who I really liked at Hastings was Ms. Laura Rice, an English teacher. She was really friendly and had a kind heart. I'm not sure what it was that she was teaching the class, because I was too busy looking around the room. But the way she was teaching the class was nice.

If she asked them a question, the kids would raise their hands and wait to be called on. They had a lot of respect for her explaining detail after detail. At Hastings the teachers seemed so close to their students, and they took time out to show them something they didn't understand.

I think school would have been different for me if I had lived in a nice suburb like Hastings, because I would probably have learned a whole lot more. It's not that I didn't learn much in my school—it's just that when I had trouble, the teachers didn't help me as much as they could have. That was a problem for me and most of the students in my school.

Still, Hastings isn't perfect. Most students said they're happy with the school because they're learning a lot there. But many also said that the school is too small, and that it's not diverse enough. The school has only 300 kids, and when I was there, I saw only five black kids and one Hispanic kid. I thought the black kids might feel a little uncomfortable because most of the school is White.

I would feel uncomfortable there myself, because I'm not used to being around a lot of white people. There are no white people in my neighborhood, and I only knew one white guy in my school. But Michael, one of the few black kids I met, said he doesn't really feel like his race stands out.

"I might have felt weird if I just moved here in 10th grade, but it doesn't bother me, because I grew up with a lot of the kids in this school," he said. "You just grow up and get used to it."

I was pretty impressed with Michael. He has a 90 average and he is taking honors and AP classes, and he plays on three sports teams during the year. And he plans to go away to college next year. I think that's good, because it's important to show that black kids can do that, too.

> *I live in the projects, and they're not a nice place to grow up.*

I think part of the reason Michael does so well in school is because there are no distractions. His neighborhood is quiet and his school is quiet. Michael just goes to football or basketball practice, and then he goes home and studies.

"My street is quiet," Michael said. "After school, no one's around."

My neighborhood is not peaceful like Michael's. I live in the projects, and they're not a nice place to grow up. In Michael's neighborhood you can leave your belongings outside and not worry about anyone stealing them. In the projects you can't even leave a child alone outside with all the stuff that goes on.

Now, not everybody wants or can afford to live in the suburbs, but we should have schools that are as good as Hastings High School here in the city. We should complain to the governor or the mayor, and protest to the Department of Education because of the way they're neglecting the schools in

From Dropout to Achiever

the poor communities, which need help the most.

Poor kids need better schools than wealthy kids, because without an education, what have they got? Nothing. And if they've got nothing, then how will they survive? I'm sure the majority of the people in the suburbs would agree with me.

The city should clean up our schools and the government should stop being so cheap. If I had everybody's ears, I would tell them to think of other people besides themselves for once. Besides, if city students don't get a good education, it's only going to cause problems for everyone in the long run.

Dean wrote this story when he was 19. After high school he joined the U.S. Army and served in the Middle East as a member of the 1st Cavalry Division during Operation Iraqi Freedom.

Real Smart

By Amber Grof

My handwriting gradually slowed as the minutes ticked by. I looked across the bleak room and stared longingly at my bed. I had covered it with stuff that would be uncomfortable to lie on, so sleep wouldn't tempt me from my work.

I rolled my eyes with frustration at the thought of the three hours spent dusting, sweeping, and finally watering all of my foster mother's damn plants. Crap! It was already midnight and I still had my Chinese and cryptology homework to do. My heavy eyelids begged me to put them to rest. I placed my head on top of my folded arms. My alarm shook me from my slumber six hours later.

This was my life at Bard High School Early College, where you graduate with not only a high school diploma, but also a two-year college degree. When I first learned of Bard in the 8th grade, it seemed amazing. I imagined being halfway done with college at the age of 18, awaiting admission to Harvard, my writing already published in well-known magazines. I had it all planned out in my dreams.

Bard had very high standards. They wanted the smartest of the smart, straight A's only, thank you. At the time, I thought that straight A's was what being smart was all about.

After I received my acceptance letter from Bard, I was ecstatic. I was one of only five from my junior high school who had been selected. All of my teachers were proud of me and I had a huge smile on my face. Bard became my golden opportunity to prove myself.

And I did. Bard helped me build my self-esteem. When the school year began, I had already been in foster care for a couple of years and I had just transferred to a new foster home. I was still adjusting to the bitter attitude of my foster mother, who saw me as little more than her maid. My biological parents were never that encouraging, either.

> **At the time, I thought that straight A's was what being smart was all about.**

Though I was upset about being placed in care, I hoped that my new foster parents would be different. But I was too hopeful. So I started putting all of my energy into excelling at Bard. It helped take my mind off my troubles at home.

But Bard was much more demanding than it seemed at first. In junior high, I was a master at slacking off. I had the smarts and never had to put in any effort. My 8th grade teachers would applaud my excellent essays, clueless that I had quickly scribbled them on my way to school. When I tried to pull that off at Bard, I realized that I could fail. After I earned 60% on my first Chinese quiz, I had to be tutored. I felt stupid as my teacher lectured me for 50 minutes.

But at first this motivated me. I poured myself into my studies and scheduled appointments with my teachers to get extra help with my work. My efforts paid off in my grades, and I no longer heard the constant criticism from my foster mother. My teachers now praised me.

I felt vindicated after seeing my report card. My B average was proof that I was more than my foster mother's maid. But I wanted her to admit it, too—I needed her to say I was smart, that I was capable of doing things. I needed support from her that she would just not provide. I felt alone and ignored.

When I left foster care and went back to my birth mother during my sophomore year, I thought things would change. Maybe our time apart had given my mother a push to improve herself. It hadn't, though, and I became angry about it.

We always argued. My mother frustrated me more than my foster mother ever had. After our arguments, I would be too fused up to care about anything. I would throw my books aside and go to sleep. My anger showed in my grades at Bard, and my teachers began to notice a change in my attitude. My work was either poorly done or not done at all.

I spoke with a friend about my problems, and she told me about emancipation—if the court granted it, I could live independently even though I was underage. With her help, I learned a lot about the process. I started developing a plan for supporting myself.

After a lot of paperwork and constant talks with my caseworker, I was finally emancipated at age 16. Because I couldn't afford a place on my own I would remain living with my mother, but I paid my own way, including my share of the rent. Emancipating myself meant I was no longer obligated to follow my mother's rules. I was free to make my own schedule, which was important because I had many responsibilities, including my first job, as a sales associate at a clothing store.

I wasn't able to fully support myself working part-time for minimum wage. Most of my paychecks went toward paying rent.

From Dropout to Achiever

At times, I would eat at my aunt's house because I couldn't buy food. Still, I was my own adult. I was struggling, but being independent felt great. It was much more agreeable than living under my mother's rules or a stranger's.

I started working more and more hours: I would go to school at 9 in the morning, rush straight to work at 2:45, and finally reach home around 10:30 at night. I was too exhausted to get any of my schoolwork done, especially when my mom and I argued.

> **Through my new school, I got several media internships that let me network with journalists and activists.**

For the second time, school went on the back burner. I couldn't seem to balance being a student at Bard with everything else. And I had trouble trusting people enough to open up about my personal problems. I had no one to talk to at Bard. I could complain to my peers about my frustrations with school, but I never felt comfortable telling them my issues at home. I felt like I was living in two worlds: one where I was a struggling student, and the other where I was a struggling daughter.

During my junior year my guidance counselor and I began meeting weekly, hoping to find a solution to my struggles. He suggested getting a job that would pay more and offer me a better schedule, so I could stay on top of my schoolwork.

I took his advice, and found a new job that was amazing. It had flexible hours, but more importantly it inspired me. I was a program associate at a community center that helps young women build leadership skills. I was shown ways to help make change in the world through activism—by fighting for women's rights, ending poverty, and other causes I was passionate about. I learned more there than I ever had at Bard.

But as the months passed, I still couldn't manage my schoolwork. It was all just too much.

My assistant principal was known for helping students leave

Bard if they were doing poorly. She gave them the extra push they needed to transfer out. So when I walked into my guidance counselor's office and found her there after mid-term report cards were mailed out, I immediately became tense and worried. After we touched on my struggles, she cut to the chase.

"Well, how do you feel you're doing here?" And there it was. I knew what she meant. So I said what she wanted me to say. I told her that I was struggling way too much. That maybe Bard was no longer for me. That I should leave. I knew I had to leave, but I just didn't want to admit it yet. With apologetic smiles on their faces, my counselor and assistant principal spoke to me about my options for transferring.

Leaving Bard was harder than emancipation. Bard represented my capabilities, my intelligence. If I couldn't finish Bard, what did that say about me? How smart could I be if I didn't graduate from there? What colleges would want me now? It was hard, but I knew I either had to transfer or worry about getting kicked out because of poor grades. I decided to transfer in the fall to a high school where students earn credits by participating in both internships and in-class studies.

At the end of the summer my mother decided to kick me out, so I moved in with a roommate just as I was starting at my new school.

My new teachers acted as if they were in a room with illiterate 6th graders and the students played the role perfectly. Students didn't seem to care if they passed or failed. They would lounge around the classroom, fall asleep, text, and drive me nuts.

I became bitter and thoughts of being back at Bard crept into my head. If I had applied myself harder, I would still be in there and wouldn't be regretting my transfer.

I worried about my education. My Bardian friends would complain about their overload of homework as I sat wondering why my new teachers never gave us work to take home. At the end of my first Chinese class, I nearly cried. I'd spent three very long and hard years studying Mandarin, only to watch my teacher incorrectly pronounce basic phrases.

By the end of the first quarter, I decided to make some changes. I knew I needed to be more careful when selecting classes and internships. I needed classes where I was not the only attentive student, and internships where I would be doing more than answering the phone all day.

If I was going to get something from this school, I'd have to push for it. So I spoke with the teachers and got insight on the courses they were teaching.

In a strange way, I realized that many things had actually been handed to me at Bard. All I had needed to do was attend the classes and study. At my new school, I had to take the initiative and do all the work for myself. Having to take that extra step helped me to start discussions with both teachers and students and, in turn, learning became more enjoyable.

I wasn't able to take on everything Bard had to offer, but I learned a lot from my struggle there. By leaving Bard, I was able to expand my options in ways I never imagined. Through my new school, I got several media internships that let me network with journalists and activists at radio stations, magazines, and television stations, something I would have previously ignored because of my studies. I felt prepared for college—and for life—in ways that I hadn't been at Bard.

The bright screen of my laptop strained my eyes. It was two in the morning and I should have been sleeping Yet my mind was buzzing with excitement.

I clicked out of the website about Sierra Leone. I had been researching the organization in Africa where I'd be volunteering after high school, thanks to some connections I made through my job at the community center. Now I knew what the sleep-away camp in Sierra Leone looked like—an abundance of tents, with children running around to different workshops and activities, smiles wide across their faces.

Real Smart

Sierra Leone had just ended an intense civil war, and I could only imagine what those children and their families had gone through and what joy the kids would get at the camp. I was looking forward most to the writing workshops there—I couldn't wait to teach the kids and then write stories about my experiences.

As I lay down, my imagination went wild thinking about the amazing things I might encounter on my trip. I couldn't wrap my brain around it—I was going to Sierra Leone. I was actually going to volunteer my time in Africa. How was that possible?

A text message from a friend at Bard complaining about her 10-page paper brought me back to the present. I closed my eyes, all the more reassured my transfer out of that school was for the best. Being "smart" now had a whole new meaning.

Amber was in high school when she wrote this story.
She later attended college in New York City.

A School Where I Can Be Myself

By Wilber Valenzuela

"F--got! Queer!"

It was my sophomore year in high school. I had just finished up my last mid-term exam and was heading for the bus when I heard yelling. I turned around and saw a whole crowd of people running after me.

"F--got! Homo!"

I started running but it wasn't long before they got me. They tried to hit me but a lady driving by in a car started yelling, "The cops, the cops!" The kids disappeared.

That wasn't the first time I was harassed because of my sexuality. My fellow students hurled insults at me all the time. One day I walked into class and saw "Hello f--got" written on the board. I was so embarrassed that day. I was too ashamed to tell

A School Where I Can Be Myself

anyone about what had happened. I had no friends at that school, no one to turn to. It got to the point where I felt it was wrong to be a homosexual. I used to hide my feelings and keep quiet. I was afraid that anything I said or did would give the others more "proof" that I was gay. School had turned into hell.

Other students had hurt me emotionally many times and I could deal with that. But once I realized that they wanted to hurt me physically, that's when I drew the line. After that crowd of people chased me and I just barely escaped getting beaten up, I was too scared to go back to school. I told a friend about the incident and he said I should transfer to another school. But I figured that no matter where I went, some people would still be homophobic and prejudiced. I didn't know what to do.

Later that week I found out about a support group for gay teenagers called Gay and Lesbian Youth of New York (GLYNY). I went to one of their meetings and told them about what had happened to me. They gave me information about the Harvey Milk School, an alternative high school for gay, lesbian, and bisexual students. I had never heard of it before. I felt relieved to hear that such a school existed. I felt they could help me since I had a lot of questions about myself.

I called the school and they gave me an appointment for an interview. Part of me was frightened about meeting new people, making new friends, and how my mother would react to

One day I walked into class and saw "Hello f--got" written on the board.

my decision to go to an all gay school. But I knew I couldn't go back to my old high school and I didn't have any time to lose since I wanted to start the next semester at a new school.

When I arrived for my interview I saw a poster of a group of teenagers and the words, "You are not alone." I had been feeling down and seeing that poster made me feel better. During the interview I had to talk about my reasons for wanting to go to the school and give a brief biography of myself. The next step was a 10-day probation period, during which the staff finds out what your academic needs are and how interested you are in learning.

Harvey Milk was small, with only a few dozen students. Everyone was very friendly and made me feel as if they were my second family. We talked to the teachers on a first name basis, which made us feel closer to them. I liked that I never had to say, "Good morning, Mr. Ashkinazy," but simply, "Hi, Steve."

> Back at my old high school, I couldn't be myself. But now I feel comfortable wearing a T-shirt that says, "I'm not gay, but my boyfriend is."

Everything about the school was different from what I was used to. Since everyone was at a different level, we did a lot of our work independently. My teacher would give me an assignment sheet and a book. After each assignment, I would go to him and he would teach me anything I didn't understand. After three periods of individual classes, we had two periods of group classes. These were different every day and covered topics like health, law, dance, and theater.

Going to the school was like therapy for me. I learned more than just math and history—I also learned about survival. Suddenly my ideas about gays changed. It wasn't like my father had told me. Not all gay men wore leather and tight jeans—that was only the stereotype. At Harvey Milk, all the students were different. Some kids dressed conservatively, others dressed punk. Some were drag queens, but they didn't wear heavy makeup like I thought they would.

I also learned about sexuality, AIDS, and safe sex, topics that my other school didn't dare talk about. My teacher and two of my other friends were infected with the HIV virus and they taught me from their experiences. I learned about testing, counseling, and living with AIDS. Safe sex kits were always available.

A School Where I Can Be Myself

Going to the Harvey Milk School helped me understand myself and made me more confident about my identity. For the first time, I felt like part of a community. I felt I could talk to anyone about my feelings without having to hide things or lie. I also became more aware of the political issues that affect me as a young gay man. Now I pay more attention to the news and current events.

I also became more outspoken and proud. Back at my old high school, I felt like I couldn't be myself. I remember one day I wore a Madonna T-shirt to school and someone said, "Only f--gots like Madonna." I put that T-shirt in the back of my closet and never wore it to school again. But now I feel comfortable wearing T-shirts that let people know who I am, including one that says, "I'm not gay, but my boyfriend is."

I graduated from the Harvey Milk School last June. Going there changed my life, and my memories of that experience will live forever.

Wilber was 18 when he wrote this story. He later graduated from the School for International Training in Vermont. He has worked as an administrative assistant, and currently works in housing.

No More Hand-Holding

By Edgar Lopez

I sat in the back of the bus next to my friend Kevin. We were on our way to Philadelphia to visit colleges with our 8th grade class, and I was happy to be away from school for the next four days. When girls sat down next to us to wait for the bathroom, I went with the old-fashioned move: the yawn and act like I'm stretching to put my arm around them. "When are we gonna go out, baby?" I asked one girl.

The main purpose of the trip was to give us a taste of college life and introduce us college professors and students. But for us students, the real purpose was to escape from school and parents, and to have fun during the long bus rides and in the hotels. Or so I thought.

We arrived at Lincoln University, our first destination, around noon. It looked like a fun place to be. Students were studying on the lawns and hanging out with their friends. I noticed some were still wearing pajamas, or shorts and flip-flops. I pointed out to one of my teachers that a successful educational institution did not have to require uniforms like ours did, and she just smiled and shook her head.

The student cafeteria was unlike anything I'd ever seen at any school. If you wanted a sandwich you could have that, or if you wanted pizza or chicken or pasta, they had it. At lunch, my friends and I grabbed a lot of everything. I'd heard that one of the hardest parts of going to college was missing home-cooked meals, but this seemed like a good substitute.

After lunch we went outside and gathered by some benches to listen to a group of college students speak. I was toward the back of the group, playing around with my friends and half-paying attention. "Not another boring talk," I thought.

Everything the students said, I had heard before: "College is fun but you have to balance your school life and social life," and "All you do in college is read, so be prepared for it," and "Buy yourself an audio recorder because college professors don't write on the board."

When my classmate Sandra (not her real name) raised her hand, I shook my head. She loved to show off her "immense" vocabulary. "What was the most perplexing experience you faced in the transition from high school to college?" she asked.

> **I didn't know how to get things done without that extra push from teachers.**

"I think having the freedom is a problem, because if you aren't serious it becomes very easy to fail," said one of the college students. That wouldn't be a problem for me, I thought. I knew how to stay focused.

"Having to buy all your materials is the hardest part because in high school, textbooks and handouts are given to you," answered a tall Hispanic student. I knew about having to purchase your own materials, so that wasn't a shock either.

From Dropout to Achiever

My teacher's nephew Michael, an African-American freshman, was next. "The hardest thing for me was not having teachers who were close to me. I went to a small school in Manhattan like you guys, where all the teachers were supportive and gave students that extra push to succeed. They don't do that here. All they want is their tuition money," he said.

Suddenly, I was like, "Whoa." He seemed just like us—a young male from Brooklyn. That connection allowed me to see for the first time the situation I might face in a few years. And it terrified me.

My school, which I've attended since 6th grade, is small and all the students and teachers know each other well. I was a decent student but I was lazy and held my work on cruise control. My teachers often pushed me to do better and offered a lot of extra help. I'd grown accustomed to that nurturing and expected it to continue as I got older.

Hearing how different college would be from someone with an experience similar to mine made me scared I might be unsuccessful there. I didn't know how to get things done without that extra push from teachers. I looked around and saw no one else moved by his words. Was I the only one who got the message? It felt like I was in the movie *Clockstoppers* and everyone but me was stuck in time. I wanted to ask him more questions, but the students had to leave.

Three days later, the long bus ride home to Brooklyn gave me a chance to reflect on my fear. I decided I needed to start working more independently now, so that by the time college came around, I'd be ready. But who was going to help me get to a point of self-reliance? Because ironically, I knew I could not become self-reliant alone. I felt I needed to slowly experience independence and grow accustomed to it.

I decided to go to the root of the problem, which was my dependence on a substitute teacher in our school, Ms. Stevenson. She was a good teacher and students could talk to her about

No More Hand-Holding

anything. She felt we all had great potential and she often stayed after school to give us extra help. I decided I had to ask her if she could help me become more independent.

Two days after we returned from the trip, I nervously walked down the stairs toward Ms. Stevenson's office. I didn't want my request to backfire and one of my most supportive teachers no longer be there for me or, even worse, have her think I was ungrateful for all her help. I knew what I needed, but I wasn't sure what I wanted.

"Ms. Stevenson, may I please speak to you?" I said, standing in the doorway of her office.

"Sure Edgar, what's wrong?" she said. She must have figured it was important because I wasn't known to miss lunch over a conversation.

I started out by telling her what the college students had told us on the trip.

"Ms. Stevenson, I need to learn how to approach problems with my schoolwork on my own. I really appreciate all the help you give me, but if I don't get used to doing stuff on my own now, by the time college comes around I'm going to be in trouble," I said.

I was relieved when she said, "I understand and I'm glad you've decided to do this." Later that day, we met and set up a plan.

Her first idea was to stop checking on me. Normally, Ms. Stevenson asked teachers for progress reports of students she knew could do better. She would often come by my class and give me a mad look if she saw me playing around. I knew that look meant "get to work," and I counted on it to get focused.

We agreed that if she no longer did that, it would force me to get focused on my own. We also agreed that I would stop going to her for help with schoolwork unless I made an extra effort on my own first. It was a good plan.

Unfortunately, it didn't work. Right away, I took advantage of our deal and became more of a slacker than ever. I walked

From Dropout to Achiever

around in the hallway during class because I knew Ms. Stevenson wouldn't be checking on me. I knew I wasn't achieving my goal of self-reliance, but slacking off was like an addiction. Besides, I was confident I could perform on the tests, so my grades would be fine.

Then my report card arrived in June. My average had plummeted about 10 points for the first time ever. I felt horrible. It made me feel that I couldn't do this alone, and I felt even less confident in my ability to perform in college. But I told myself that nobody just changes overnight. I had to keep trying.

I told myself that nobody just changes overnight. I had to keep trying.

"You're back," Ms. Stevenson said when I appeared in her office again.

"Yeah, have you seen my report card?" I said.

"I knew this would happen. Do you see what I've been trying to keep you away from?"

That report card turned out to be a good reality check. Now I knew what would happen if I wasn't self-reliant. I needed to get serious about becoming a more independent student.

Over the next year, my freshman year in high school, there were many more obstacles on my path to self-reliance. I failed biology my first semester and did poorly in math.

But all the work I handed in was mine alone. It felt good that I wasn't going to Ms. Stevenson for help. After I did badly that first semester, I decided to cut out the baby in me and do what I needed to do to improve my grades.

I developed a study schedule. Every day I devoted no less than 30 minutes to every subject I received homework for, instead of not studying at all, like before. Instead of complaining that I didn't know about a topic, I began to read more about it.

And instead of spending money on expensive sneakers or clothes, I invested in myself. I went to Barnes & Noble and found biology textbooks that targeted our statewide exams and went into more depth than my schoolbooks.

No More Hand-Holding

By the end of my freshman year, I realized I was working independently. My study habits were now a part of my routine. My greatest moment was seeing my report card that June.

I had done better in all of my classes. I was most excited to see an 85 for my French class, the hardest class I had. Through my own persistence I had improved my grade by 15 points.

Now I never expect anyone to hold my hand and do my work for me. I'm not a machine that knows everything, but I don't automatically run for help anymore when I can't comprehend something. This has helped me prepare for the real world, during college and after it.

Edgar was 17 when he wrote this story.

How I Graduated

By Angi Baptiste

I remember my first day in high school. I was scared and nervous, walking back and forth looking for the classrooms and going through a lot of confusion that really made me want to cry. I think that a lot of kids go through that on their first day of high school.

It was hard at first keeping up with the classes and the teachers, especially in math. I always fell asleep in math because it was boring and I hated it. Other times I didn't care because I used to put myself down all the time, and I used to think I was never gonna make it. Those were the kind of thoughts that used to go through my mind. It made me say to myself, "Why bother?"

It took me a while to stop thinking that way by realizing this was my future that I was messing with. If other people could do it, so could I. And I started to think of one thing someone once told me: "Never say never until you try."

From there I decided to make a change. I started studying for every test and going over my math when I wasn't doing anything. When I finally made some progress in math, everything started to go well for me. I started doing my homework for every class, because the teachers were tired of hearing, "I left the homework on the kitchen table by mistake because I was rushing for school."

The teachers were simply asking me to do my homework and my work when I came to class. That's not a hard thing to do, right? I was just lazy.

It was hard to stop being lazy. Going to math class at 8:30 in the morning wasn't my style. I would say to myself, "This week I'm gonna cut this class and that class, and next week I'll start going to all my classes." It took me a while to finally make up my mind to go to all my classes.

That's what my main problem was—laziness. But I fought it because I knew that I didn't want to get left back. I didn't

> *I couldn't concentrate in school. I used to think about the past, about all the things that I went through.*

want to disappoint my foster parents, because they believed that I was gonna make it. That would have hurt me very bad, to let them and everybody else down. Most of all, I wouldn't be proud of myself or forgive myself for not trying hard enough.

My other problem was not being able to concentrate in school. I couldn't stop thinking about the problems I had in foster care. I couldn't stop worrying about what was gonna happen to me in the future after leaving foster care, whether I would be dead or alive by the age of 20, or make it to see tomorrow.

But after a while I realized that I had to work hard. Every time I got my report card, I knew I had to be more serious in order to reach my goals in life. To have a good future, you have to have a high school diploma and a college degree.

From my hard work I made it to the 10th grade. By then I

knew everybody, every teacher and every kid in school. But I had gone back to cutting classes. I didn't do it as often as I used to. I would only cut a class that I didn't feel like going to. I didn't get into the habit of cutting classes every day because I would have regretted it later on.

When I started 11th grade, I was still going to school and doing what I had to do. But in the 12th grade, I started to panic because I was afraid that I wasn't gonna make it. I couldn't concentrate in school again. I used to think about the past, about all the things that I went through.

A lot of things were on my mind. That's when I started to believe what my father used to say: "You'll never graduate, because you're nothing."

These were the thoughts on my mind 24/7 that I couldn't stop worrying about. I realized I needed to concentrate more when I saw my first report card from my senior year. I was disappointed with myself for thinking about other things instead of school. I wanted to do well and graduate to prove my dad wrong.

So I decided to take night school and work extra hard. My foster parents stood by my side and got me a tutor to help me with my math three days a week. I also had tutoring in school for the state tests two days a week. Boy, I started to get tired of it, but I kept going, even though I didn't like tutoring, because I knew it was for the best.

The hardest thing for me about going to school and being in foster care was when my friends would talk about their families and how cool they are. That would make me jealous, because that's not the family I have. And my friends would go on and on about it. Man, that used to make me so sick. It's like they would continue on about their families just to torture me. Only a few of my friends knew I was in foster care.

Hearing my friends talking about these things used to make me angry and depressed. A lot of time in class I would be in another world, just thinking about how unhappy I was with myself and my house (even though at least I wasn't living on the streets, and I thank God for that). It's just that I wasn't happy in my foster home. So going to school was much better than being in my house, and when school was over and it was time for me to go home, I would get very depressed.

School was like my real home because everybody there showed that they cared about how I was doing. When I needed someone to talk with, the teachers were always there to listen and to give me advice. I think the reason my teachers were always there for me was because they knew my situation and they were trying to help me and I think that was very sweet of them.

The day after I graduated I finally called my dad. I told him that I got my diploma, and he cried.

The teachers cared about others, too. But I had the most attention. I guess it's because they felt bad for me because I'm in foster care and because of the problems I was going through. Most of them wanted me to succeed.

So after school my social studies teacher would give me extra help in social studies. If I missed a day I would get in trouble. That showed me that she cared a lot about my education.

When my teacher told me that I passed everything and that I was graduating, I was so very happy. On the day of my graduation, my foster family was there cheering for me. They were proud of me and I was proud of myself that I made it.

The day after I graduated I finally called my dad, who I never used to keep in contact with. I told him that I got my diploma. He cried because he wasn't expecting it. He thought I was a loser. He was expecting my sister Ingrid to graduate, but instead my sister turned out to be the dropout.

I'm angry at my sister for the fact that she gave up and stopped trying, but that doesn't mean that I don't still love her. She's my big sister and she's in my heart. She's a very big part of me.

From Dropout to Achiever

My advice to others—I just want to say never think any less of yourself because you're in foster care and never feel that you're never gonna make it. Because it's not true. If you work hard, everything will be OK. Just take everything one day at a time. Never think low of yourself or say that you're never gonna make it. You have the power to make things happen for yourself.

Angi was 18 when she wrote this story. After high school, she worked at Bloomingdale's and had a child.

Lost in a Big School

By Danica Webb

On the first day of high school, I felt like a little fish in a tank full of sharks. To get in the building, students had to wait in line to go through a security check. It made school seem more like a maximum security prison than a learning facility.

Inside, the four-story building was huge and crowded, which turned my first-day excitement into anxiety. I had to push through a sea full of people who were hanging out in the hallways just to get to class.

Pretty soon, I found out that some teachers would lock you out if you didn't make it by the late bell, even if the bell rang as you were approaching the classroom door. You would have to spend the period in a room on the first floor called "lockout" along with all the other late kids.

From Dropout to Achiever

One morning as I was going through the security check, the guard stopped me. "I found something," the security guard said as my bag was going through the scanning machine. She reached into my bag and pulled out a pair of scissors.

"Oh that? That's not even mine," I said. I had borrowed the scissors from a school staff member, had accidentally taken them home, and was now returning them.

"This is contraband," she said.

"I didn't know that; if I did I wouldn't have brought it," I said.

"Ignorance of the rules is not my problem," she said. I ended up getting suspended even though the staff member confirmed that they were her scissors.

I was angry. This showed me how messed up the school system was, and how it lacked compassion for students. I wasn't exactly a saint, of course; I'd been suspended before. But this wasn't a justifiable suspension, like the times when I refused to give up my phone, or acted out in class, or got into fights.

The discipline system was discouraging, but I also became overwhelmed with schoolwork. By the second semester of freshman year, my effort in school started lagging. I felt the teachers weren't helping me enough. When I needed help, they were focused on the bad kids in class.

My school seemed more like a maximum security prison than a learning facility.

Even my counselor, Mr. Lopez, never took the time to meet with me or talk about my future. For example, he didn't tell me about the PSAT. He hadn't even given me the right classes so that I would be on track to graduate—though I didn't realize that until much later. I asked other kids about him, and they told me they'd had similar experiences.

I stuck it out, but my disappointment continued. I can't blame everything on my school; I had some issues at home, too. I was living with an alcoholic uncle and another verbally abusive uncle who was loud and destructive. The combination of home prob-

Lost in a Big School

lems and lack of care from the school sent my situation from bad to worse.

I stopped applying myself because I felt no one cared. Even though education was valued in my home, no one helped me with homework. At school, if I asked for help, teachers would dryly tell me to go to after-school tutoring, and no student at that school wanted to stay after school. No teacher took the time to tell me that I wasn't passing the class or to give me options to improve my grades.

During my junior year, my grandfather talked to me about changing schools. Though he was in poor health, he walked up three flights of stairs just to talk to my counselor about me transferring. I felt good that he cared enough to come, but I wasn't ready for change. Being at my high school was like being in a bad relationship: You know that things aren't good but you try to stick it out, hoping for better and afraid to change.

My fear kept me from taking my grandfather's advice. I thought I could overcome the obstacles. I changed my mind when my grandfather died. I wanted to make him proud. I also wanted to be better than my mother, who never graduated from high school.

But when I realized I wasn't going to graduate at the end of my senior year, I had a discussion with my new guidance counselor, Ms. Martin. She told me about alternative schools that can help students catch up if they're behind in credits. Now I was open to it; I felt like I had to do something to make up for lost time and get a high school diploma.

Ms. Martin actually took the time to get to know me. She would call me from class just to see how I was doing. I felt that she wanted me to succeed.

I walked into Ms. Martin's office ready to advocate for myself and transfer schools.

"I don't think this school is good for me. I don't see me graduating in this type of environment."

"Well, I told you if you wanted there is a list of schools you can go to that might be better for you, so you can get on track to graduating," she said.

"OK," I said, "What do I have to do?"

She explained that I'd have to bring my guardian to the new school, along with my transcript, I.D., and proof of address. Queens Academy was the one closest to me, so I decided to check it out the next morning. Ms. Martin said Queens Academy was a small school where I could get more support. "Good luck," said Ms. Martin. "I have a feeling you'll do well there."

The next morning my dad and I went to Queens Academy. I felt the same excitement I had when I first started high school. I hoped that I could leave the old me behind and have a fresh start.

Finding a supportive school environment has changed my attitude toward education. Now I really apply myself.

They explained that the environment was different from larger high schools. It seemed like a safer, more home-like environment where the staff were more like family than robots. They were friendlier than the teachers at my old school and eager to teach us. I decided to enroll.

One thing I liked about Queens Academy was that we were told to address staff by their first names. To me this made them more down to earth. Instead of dictators, they were more like colleagues.

In fact, I felt like I could talk to my new teachers about anything, like college and possible careers. I wasn't afraid to ask for help if I didn't understand something, and I felt that they cared about me enough to help me until I did understand. At my old school, I don't think my teachers even noticed if I was there or not.

Queens Academy also had something called a "good phone call." Instead of just calling your home if you were bad, teachers also called to let your parents know that you were doing well in class. All of this positive reinforcement made me a better student. It built my confidence so I felt that I could succeed in school if I just kept working hard.

My counselor Susan was very friendly and motherly. She always had a smile and a kind word. She even made sure to congratulate me when I made the honor roll. It felt good to know that she cared and saw that I was trying my best at the school.

Finding a supportive school environment has changed my attitude toward education. I found myself really applying myself, raising my hand to participate, and coming to school on time every day. I did my homework and finished assignments on time.

After the first term, I got one of the best report cards I'd ever received since elementary school, with a 95 average. I was ecstatic that my hard work was paying off and I was closer to getting a high school diploma. The report card proved that I wasn't dumb and that if I worked hard enough, the outcome would be positive. Now, I finally feel like I am in charge of my destiny.

Danica graduated from high school after writing this article.

What's Wrong With Reading?

By Anthony Turner

Recently I was "caught" reading at McDonald's by a group of kids at my school. I say "caught" because many of my peers consider reading to be a lame activity. They think it's only something that geeks do.

But there I was, reading *Med Head* by James Patterson, a mystery/suspense author, when they strolled by. One girl named Tiffany walked up and said "Is that a..." she rubbed her eyes and acted like she couldn't believe what I was doing. "...book?" she finished in a sarcastic, incredulous way.

I shrugged and said, "Reading is really good for you. Maybe you should try it." She snorted and said "How about never." Then she bent over and touched my cheek and turned away, leaving with the others.

It wasn't the first time that something like that happened.

What's Wrong With Reading?

When I occasionally go to the library, kids ask me why I'm reading. "It's a library, that's what you're supposed to do!" They just shake their heads.

I don't understand why they think reading is dumb. To me, being a reader means being open-minded, intellectual, and willing to learn new things. Reading has helped empower me and teach me important things that I might not have known about otherwise, like African history or world leaders. Also it's just fun to get into the story, especially if the writing is witty, and learn new vocabulary that I can use later in a conversation.

But black youth culture prizes guys who play ball, bag girls, dance, and rap. Simply reading a book is considered passive or introverted. Or it's considered a "white thing"—something black kids, especially black boys, shouldn't be caught doing if they want to be popular. Unfortunately, I think some kids hold themselves back academically for those reasons. I know I feel slightly wary around books after hearing my peers say that people who read have no lives.

Reading a book is considered passive or introverted. Or it's considered a 'white thing.'

When I participate in class and answer all the questions, I get laughed at. The same thing happens when I get caught reading for fun. So sometimes I try to cover up my "smarts" by making jokes or looking disinterested in class. After all, I don't want to be considered a geek or nerd for simply reading a book. I want to be known for being outgoing just like most of the "cool kids" are.

My school is in BedStuy, Brooklyn. BedStuy is a tough place. I usually see garbage on the floor, graffiti on walls, overturned garbage cans, and kids looking to make fast money. It's simply not the type of neighborhood where you smile and say, "Wow, I think I'll do great here." Many kids don't see themselves striving higher than a high school education because of the heavy influence of the streets, where drug dealing and other illegal activities are common. The kids and even the adults don't care that much about education—which means they don't care about reading.

It was different for me. Reading was something I always seemed to be around. My mom, grandparents, and other adults who I visited often had books lying around. I enjoyed getting into a book and trying to imagine how the characters felt. I remember liking the book *Tyrell* by Coe Booth because the main character was a young black kid hoping to find his way through the streets, and in the meantime trying to do something productive. I could identify with him. *Flight*, by Sherman Alexie, is another favorite.

My mom, along with other adults in my life, always stressed that education was "the key to all things." She was a college dropout, and I guess she wanted a better life for me. She told me that education can get you places, so I took education, and reading, as a way to improve myself.

Being able to enjoy the simple pleasures of reading also allowed me to dig into black history and understand my ancestors. For example, I learned that when slavery was legal in the U.S., many black people weren't even allowed to read or write. Black people were kept ignorant on purpose.

Slave holders opposed slave literacy because they were concerned that literate slaves would convince others to read and write, and as they gained power through knowledge, they would revolt. If slaves got caught reading or writing, they could be viciously flogged or even killed.

Frederick Douglass, one of my most inspiring African-American heroes, was an abolitionist who gained a vast amount of knowledge by reading books even though it was against the law. Bribing white kids in his neighborhood with food, Douglass was gradually able to learn to read and empower himself.

Douglass was able to use his knowledge to advocate for other African-Americans who felt lost and powerless in the world of slavery. He even became President Abraham Lincoln's trusted

What's Wrong With Reading?

adviser on difficult political issues, such as the abolition of slavery. Reading was key to Douglass' ability to improve society.

Another important time for African-Americans was the Civil Rights Movement, when blacks tried to gain racial equality. Although slavery had been outlawed, African-Americans suffered terrible forms of discrimination and often faced violence if they tried to challenge the system.

One of the biggest inequalities of the time was education. African-Americans were forced to attend schools that had worn out textbooks, dirty rooms, and very few supplies. These obstacles set African-Americans back. Without good teachers, better textbooks, and enough supplies, the kids couldn't reach their full potential, so many stayed stuck in low-wage jobs that gave them little influence in society.

> *I took education, and reading, as a way to improve myself.*

Although many black people in the 1800s would have died to be able to read a book, and many more African-Americans struggled in the 1900s to gain equal access to education, a lot of black teens now look down on reading and writing. The freedom that our ancestors rigorously fought for is sadly being taken for granted and even laughed at.

I've tried to convince my friends that reading isn't the geeky activity they think it is, but I haven't made much progress. They don't seem to get that reading is something that actually exercises and stimulates your brain. And I still get teased for reading.

I walked into a bookstore one day after school to unwind before I headed home. Out of the corner of my eye I saw a kid from my school, Devin, who happened to be in my Advanced Placement English class. I saw him with a broom and dust pan, so I figured he worked there.

To my surprise he made a beeline right to me and demanded, "Why are you reading a book?" I blinked at him, confusion written all over my face. I hardly spoke to Devin at school so it was a surprise that he was talking to me.

From Dropout to Achiever

"I enjoy reading and it's a good way to pass the time," I said. "And what do you mean why? You make it seem like it's a bad thing."

Devin just shook his head and said, "I just don't see how anyone would read. It's a waste of time. You should be chilling with your boys, not cooped up in a bookstore." Before I could say another word he walked away, leaving me confused and wondering, yet again: Is it bad to read?

I had to remind myself that—no, it isn't. Reading helps you build up your vocabulary and learn about things outside the classroom. Reading helps you prepare for college, in the sense that you're already used to picking up a book and doing research on your own. This is especially important for African-Americans.

African-American and Hispanic males have the lowest high school graduation rates in the U.S. We need to step up our performance in order to compete. With the economy the way it is, the chances for black youth to succeed can look pretty slim, and if we don't like to read, those chances get even slimmer. So, the next time you're killing time by updating your status on Facebook or watching TV, think about reading a book instead. It helps more than you know.

Anthony was 18 when he wrote this story. He graduated from high school and now attends college in New York City.

VIDEO

Teens: Why Do You Read? Go to bit.ly/whydoyouread or scan the code.

Does Reading Make You a Nerd? Go to bit.ly/teensreading or scan the code.

You're On Your Own, Kid

By Otis Hampton

In high school, I just did what I had to do to get B's and C's. I could do that without doing my homework, so I didn't do homework. I didn't push myself to be an A student because as long as I passed and graduated, being the top student didn't matter.

I did want to go to college, though, because when I was 6, I promised my dad that I would. He died soon after that, but I wanted to keep my promise. Having an education meant the same thing to both of us: that I could use my knowledge to achieve my goals in life. One of my goals, partly because my dad taught me to write, is becoming a professional writer.

I was accepted into all six colleges that I applied to in New York City. I wanted to go to Brooklyn College to study journalism, but my mom wanted me to go to Medgar Evers College because it was closer to home. I got some federal financial aid

From Dropout to Achiever

money through both a Pell grant and a TAP (Tuition Assistance Program) award for books, transportation, and other expenses. But my mom was paying the rest, so I had to go where she said.

I took a multiple-choice placement test to determine what freshman classes I would take, and I aced it. In high school, I'd only gotten A's on tests where all the questions were multiple choice. Seeing the options on multiple-choice tests helps me remember what I read or what the teacher said in class. I've always had trouble remembering what I've read.

I signed up for math, English, history, and freshman seminar, an introduction to college life. But almost immediately, I ran into problems.

One big problem was that I didn't get my books until mid-October. The portion of my Pell grant that covered books didn't come through until then. I tried to keep up by reading what I could at the library, but without being able to take the textbooks home with me to study, I fell behind in my classes.

My advice is to stay on top of your financial aid. Keep reminding the financial aid office that you need your money for books, transportation, and other expenses—not just tuition. Also, ask other students to fill you in if you miss class.

Another big problem was that I wasn't used to studying. In high school, the only thing I studied was math because we got work packets to take home instead of a heavy textbook. But college math—algebra plus trigonometry—was so much more difficult than high school math. The only time I understood the work was when we did problems from the book and on the board.

I realized I needed help when I failed my very first quiz in math class. I was too embarrassed to ask the teacher for help. I wanted him to think that I really belonged in college. The free tutoring Medgar Evers offered was at the same time as my classes, so I hired a student tutor. I didn't want my mom to pay for a tutor out of her own money because she was already going through financial problems herself. I decided to use the last of my money on tutoring sessions. The tutor helped me with word problems, which were giving me the most trouble. To my relief, I passed my midterm.

The hardest parts of the semester were the final exams. I would have to study everything from Day 1 because I had missed most of the work since I hadn't gotten the books on time.

I really felt pressured now because if I didn't pass the final, then I wouldn't pass the class. In high school, you always got another chance to take Regents exams until you passed them.

I was too embarrassed to ask the teacher for help. I wanted him to think that I really belonged in college.

In high school, tests were always given at the regular class time. But not in college. Math was an evening class so I thought that the exam would take place then, but it was in the morning. I talked to my teacher about it, and to my dismay he said there was nothing he could do about it. I failed math and had to take the class over the following semester.

I got a B in freshman seminar and a D in history. For English class, I got an "NC" (Not Complete) because of an essay that was missing. That didn't sit right with me. Because my printer at home wasn't working, I had e-mailed the assignment to my teacher the night before it was due. She claimed that she never received it.

I wanted to do better in the spring semester than I did in the fall so I got some help from the education specialist at my foster care/adoption agency. She is my go-to person for questions about registering for classes or anything else college-related. With her help, I registered for the spring semester; she told me which classes I had to take over.

I also made some sacrifices. In the fall semester, I had hung out with friends during my free time and stayed up all night playing video games. At the beginning of the spring semester, I sold my video game system to pay for subway cards and I stopped hanging out with my friends as much, so I would have more time to study. Without my friends or video games to distract me, I did get more studying done. Plus, I only took three classes, nine credits instead of 12.

Despite my new discipline, the spring semester didn't go so well either. The only class I passed was English. For speech class, I had to prepare speeches and I was not ready for that. I was nervous because the professor was very strict and that made me uncomfortable. She was always criticizing the students' flaws and making it seem like we didn't know what we were doing. As for math, I just couldn't stay awake because the class was at 7 am.

Many colleges, including Medgar Evers, require students to maintain at least a 2.0 GPA to stay in school. I was close, but not quite there, so I was dismissed from school. I was disappointed in myself, and my mom was disappointed too. Most of all, I let my dad down. I had broken my promise to him, and I cried about that.

> **I vowed that Facebook and video games could wait until after I've done at least two hours of studying.**

My first-year struggles made me realize that I had a lot of growing up to do to become a successful student. For example, I need to find my own motivation for going to college that is separate from what my dad wanted, or what other relatives tell me I should be doing.

I'm trying to separate out what I want from everyone else's expectations of me. My uncle wants me to study law or "med'cine" and my mom wants me to "make something of myself." All I keep hearing from everybody else is "job" this or "bills" that. I'm tired of hearing that, but I know I need college to meet my goal of being a professional writer.

Fortunately, I was given a second chance. There is a program at Kingsborough Community College called New Start that lets you enroll with a clean slate—a brand new GPA. I sent them my college transcript and explained my situation—that I was having trouble focusing so I flunked out.

Talking to my educational adviser and others made me realize that I might have some sort of learning disability. When I pick up a book and start reading, my mind goes blank. To be honest, the only type of book that doesn't put me to sleep is a children's book. I prefer books with pictures.

High school reading was different because we did most of the reading in class and were given writing assignments about what we read. In college, I would read the assigned pages at home but would not remember or understand them.

I thought that everyone had those same struggles. But they don't, so I decided to get screened for disabilities and get help with my reading comprehension and with math.

It turns out that I don't have any learning disabilities, but I did discover that my weaknesses are test-taking and study habits. To help me improve, I decided to take advantage of tutors and education specialists and seek out their help as soon as I need it. I also vowed that Facebook and video games could wait until after I've done at least two hours of studying every day.

I've been in the New Start program for six weeks now. This time around, I scheduled my classes a month before school started instead of waiting until the last minute. I was appointed an academic counselor, and she told me what classes I was required to take. Most of them were the equivalent of the classes I took (and failed) at Medgar Evers.

A few weeks later, I took care of financial aid and got my money situation in order. I got money to buy books a week after school started, so I was in better shape for this semester. As for transportation, my mom reluctantly offered to buy me a 30-day metrocard for the first month as long as I paid her back. I even signed a contract with her.

So here I am Kingsborough Community College with a brand new slate. Four classes, 13 credits, and so far everything's going smoothly.

Otis is still struggling to take his own advice so he can succeed in college!

VIDEO

Otis's Second Chance

To see a video of Otis explaining his study tips, go to bit.ly/otis2ndchance or scan the code.

FICTION SPECIAL

Schooled

"Lionel, can you read the poem to us?"

Lionel Shephard cringed. It was the third time Mrs. Henley, his English teacher at Bluford High School, called on him today.

First she'd asked him to define what the American Dream was. Lionel joked that it was what happened when everybody in the country was sleeping. Dontrell Neeves, his classmate and friend since second grade, laughed out loud.

"You trippin,' L," he whispered.

Mrs. Henley smiled and moved on, but she returned a few minutes later, pressing him with another question. She even circled to the back row where he sat, stopping just a few feet from his desk. Her eyes beamed through her glasses like two bright headlights focused on him.

"So, as an American citizen, Lionel, what is *your* dream?"

Lionel wanted to ask her why she was always picking on him. It had been going on since he started his freshman year a month

---

This is the first chapter from *Schooled*, by Paul Langan, a novel about teens facing difficult situations like the ones you read about in this book. *Schooled* is one of many books in the Bluford Series™ by Townsend Press.

ago. Jamar Coles, his friend from the car wash where he worked weekends, would have told her off right there in the middle of class.

"Get yo' bug-eyes outta my face."

Lionel could picture Jamar shoving a desk at her and walking out in the middle of class. Of course, Jamar had dropped out of high school last year. Lionel often thought of doing that, but he knew his dad would never allow it. Neither would Mom, though she was sitting in a sandy army base on the other side of the world, too far away to do anything about it if he did.

"Basketball. I'm gonna play in the NBA one day," Lionel answered. He meant it, though half the class snickered at him.

"Yeah, me too. We all gonna play," said Rasheed Watkins from the far corner of the room. A few other students giggled.

"Why you gotta say that?" cut in Malika Shaw from the front row. "People said I wouldn't run hurdles again after I broke my ankle, but they were wrong. I'm still running."

"Whatever," Rasheed said, rolling his eyes. "He's dreamin' if he thinks he's gonna play in the NBA. Maybe smokin' something too."

"Man, I'll smoke you on the court right now," Lionel shot back.

What did Rasheed know? He wasn't there when Lionel's squad at the Greene Street Police Athletic League won the summer basketball tournament. Lionel had blocked a shot in the final seconds, allowing Greene Street to defeat the Tanner Street Titans for the first time in three years. Officer Hodden, his coach, was so happy that he'd lifted Lionel up in the middle of the court.

"You're a smart player, Lionel. Keep playin' like that and you might have a future in the sport," he'd said. It was one of the few times Lionel could remember anyone calling him smart. On the court, it was true. But school was a different story.

"Lionel? Can you read the poem to us?" Mrs. Henley repeated, snapping him from his thoughts.

118

Why wouldn't she just skip him? He could handle that, coasting in the back row, working in small groups and copying what other kids did, getting them to do the work for him. He'd been doing it for years. Hadn't she realized what his middle school teachers knew, that he wasn't the one to call on in class?

"Which poem?" Lionel asked, sitting up in his desk. He knew class was almost over.

Rasheed rolled his eyes and sucked his teeth. "I told you he's dreamin', Mrs. Henley," he said.

"Rasheed, I am about to be your nightmare," Lionel cut back.

"That's enough, gentlemen," Mrs. Henley said. "The poem's called 'Harlem,' by Langston Hughes. It's on page sixty-two."

Lionel reached down and dragged his heavy textbook off the floor. Reluctantly he flipped it open, his heart starting to pound. He hated being put on the spot in class. It made his temples hurt and his palms go clammy and cold. Sometimes, it even made it difficult to focus, like right now.

"What page again?"

"Boy, don't you listen?" Rasheed hissed.

"That's enough," Mrs. Henley repeated firmly, flashing Rasheed a look that silenced him. "Page sixty-two, Lionel."

Several students snickered. Lionel could feel the eyes of his classmates crawling over him, judging him. It was like the day back in fifth grade, before Mom's army unit was deployed, when he really started having trouble in school.

Then Mr. Grabowski, a substitute teacher in his science class, asked him to read aloud a passage about insects. Lionel had always been one of the weakest readers in class. For a time, he got extra help figuring out letters and sounds. And he used what he knew the day Mr. Grabowski called on him. But it didn't help with the word "mosquito."

"*M-m-moss*," he'd stammered, trying to make the letters on the page into sounds that made sense. "*Moss-quit-oh*," he had said finally, the word as meaningless as those countless tests he'd filled in with number two pencils each year.

"*Moss quit?!*" teased a girl next to him. Lionel could still hear how the beads at the ends of her braids clicked as she shook her head at him, her face twisted into a cruel smirk. At the time, Lionel was one of the shortest kids in class. It was years before the growth spurt that made him a wiry six-footer over the summer.

"*Boy, I think your brain just quit,*" she had mocked. The whole class erupted in laughter. Lionel's face seared with embarrassment.

"*I think you should quit talking 'cause your breath stink,*" he snapped back.

"*At least I ain't like you—too stupid for school,*" she had said before Mr. Grabowski settled them down.

Though it happened years ago, Lionel remembered the moment as if it was yesterday. One ugly word from that day still echoed in his head whenever teachers tried to push him.

Stupid.

He heard it now with Mrs. Henley leaning toward him. Maybe it was true. Lionel felt that way whenever he struggled with reading and writing.

It started back in elementary school with him always being behind his peers. But it got worse in middle school, especially after Mom left.

At the time, his teachers seemed to feel sorry for him. They said nothing when he withdrew to the back of the room with the other kids who hated school. They didn't yell as much when his homework was late or when he acted up in class. It was as if they knew that Dad was struggling to raise him and his little sister Kendra, and they didn't want to trouble him.

Lionel expected Bluford High School would be more of the same, but he was wrong. Mrs. Henley and his other teachers were constantly on his case, especially today.

"I'll read it, Mrs. Henley," said Malika from her corner seat in the second row. She glanced over at him, her hair pulled back behind her head, making her curls spill like coppery ribbons down her neck. She was someone who always answered Mrs. Henley's questions. Sometimes she seemed to bail Lionel out when he didn't have an answer.

Lionel hoped Mrs. Henley would give up on him and let Malika read.

"No, thank you, Malika. We know what your voice sounds like. I want to hear Lionel's for once," Mrs. Henley said. "Go on, Lionel."

Lionel glanced down at the open page. Words covered just half of it, so he knew the poem was short. And he'd heard Mrs. Henley say the title, so he knew what the first word was. But what about the rest?

"Why do we have to read a poem anyway?" he asked.

It's what he often did when teachers tried to get in his face: distract them, push back, waste time. But this time, he meant it. Reading out loud wasn't going to bring Mom home or allow Dad to work less or stop the bullets that killed his neighbor's grandson in his neighborhood a couple of years ago.

"It's not like this or any poem really matters when you step out of this school, Mrs. Henley," Lionel continued. "I mean maybe it matters somewhere, but not here."

Mrs. Henley nodded thoughtfully.

"That's deep, yo," Dontrell said.

"I think you and Langston Hughes might have more in common than you think, Lionel," she said with a knowing grin. "Why don't you read it and we'll see."

The class grew silent again. Lionel saw Malika looking at him. Rasheed too.

Lionel could feel tiny drops of sweat gathering on his forehead. His heart started to pound. His legs bounced nervously. He took a deep breath and looked at the words, at the first letters. He tried to focus on them, figure them out. But in his mind he could

From Dropout to Achiever

hear how childish he would sound. He could feel the embarrassment already, the laughter that was sure to rain down on him. His hands curled into fists.

Ring!

The bell signaling the end of first period blared loudly overhead. Lionel sighed with relief and closed his eyes as the class exploded into chaos. Students jumped from their desks and rushed to the hallway. He slammed his book shut and made his way toward the doorway when he heard Mrs. Henley call out behind him.

"We'll have to continue this on Monday," she announced. "Lionel, can you come here for a second please?"

Lionel cringed. Why couldn't she just leave him alone? He dragged himself to her desk on the other side of the room, looking back once to see Malika disappear down the hallway.

"I gotta go to my next class," he said.

"I know, but I just want to give you this," she said, handing him a crisp white envelope.

"What is it?"

"A letter for your parents."

"For what?!"

"Because you barely participate in class. You never handed in your first assignment, and on your last quiz you scored a 50," she explained. "I think you're capable of more, and I want your parents to know it."

"Why you gotta be like that, Mrs. Henley?" Lionel asked, thinking of how upset Dad would be to see the note. "I didn't do nothin' wrong today."

"No you didn't, but that doesn't change what I just said. I want to see you focus on your work, and I think this letter can help. It's only the first marking period. You still have time to change how this class is going, but you need to start working now, and your parents need to know that."

Lionel rolled his eyes. Dad said the same thing when Lionel

announced his plan to join the NBA the night his team won the Police Athletic League tournament.

"*You can keep messin' around on the court all you want,*" Dad had said. "*But I want to see you spend some more time worrying about school. You're getting older, and it's time you start takin' your education seriously.*"

Lionel hated Dad's words. *Messing around on the court.* It was an insult, as if he was playing a kid's game, not something serious.

"*Why you gotta talk about it like that? I can make more money playin' ball than I'll ever make in school,*" Lionel had tried to explain.

"*Yeah, Dad!*" his little sister Kendra had cheered. "*Then he can buy us a new house like on that show Phat Cribs. We could have a pool and four cars and—*"

"*That's enough, baby.*"

"*He's really good, Leroy. You should see how quick he is,*" Aunt Mimi had chimed in, bouncing her daughter, Sahara, on her knee. Aunt Mimi was Dad's younger sister. She moved in to help out right after Mom left. When Lionel started seventh grade, she announced she was pregnant, and her boyfriend was going to marry her. But that never happened.

"*Yeah, I know he's quick, Mimi, but there are a hundred quick kids a block from here. How many of 'em make it to the NBA?*"

Aunt Mimi didn't answer.

"*Whatever,*" Lionel had grumbled.

"*Don't you whatever me, boy. I'm trying to talk some sense into you. School is your ticket out of here, not basketball. Understand?*" his father had said, pointing his arm toward the barred front window that faced Cypress Street.

Lionel knew what was out there. Down the block was Kwik Cash, where strangers wandered in at all hours to sell stuff for money. Almost everything there was stolen. Further down was Discount Liquors and Tez's Lounge, a neighborhood bar with graffiti-stained stucco walls that smelled of urine. The area was dangerous, especially after dark. Some nights, gunshots cracked and popped in the distance.

"But Dad, if I go pro, we can move—"

"Enough, Lionel! What happens if you don't make it, huh? What happens if you get hurt? You'll just be another kid without an education or a future. Maybe you wind up in jail. Maybe worse. I can't have that. You understand?"

Lionel shrugged, struggling not to argue with his father.

"Yeah, I understand, Dad. But you don't," he'd added under his breath.

Now Mrs. Henley was trying to tell him the same thing.

"Okay, Mrs. Henley, I'll take the note to him," Lionel lied. He knew he'd toss the letter in the trash as soon as he left the classroom. It wouldn't be the first time.

"Good," Mrs. Henley replied. "And one last thing, Lionel. I want you to have your dad sign it. Bring it back on Monday and be ready to read your poem to the class."

Schooled, a Bluford Series™ novel, is reprinted with permission from Townsend Press. Copyright © 2002.

Want to read more? This and other *Bluford Series*™ novels and paperbacks can be purchased for $1 each at www.townsendpress.com. Or tell an adult (like your teacher) that they can receive copies of *Schooled* for free if they order a class set of 15 or more copies of *From Dropout to Achiever*. To order, visit www.youthcomm.org or call 212-279-0708 x115.

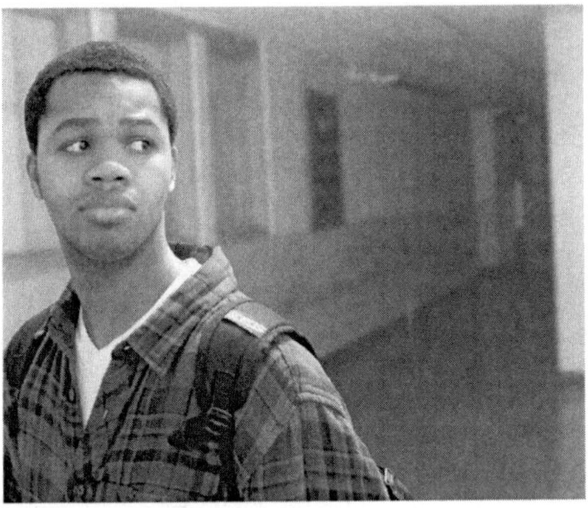

Credits

The stories in this book originally appeared in the following Youth Communication publications:

"Hiding My Talent No More," by Jesselin Rodriguez, *YCteen*, December 1996

"From Inmate to College Student," By Marlo Scott, *Represent*, Spring, 2012

"A Stranger in a Strange School," By Esther Rajavelu, *YCteen*, September/October 1995

"Will the Tortoise Win the Race?," By Eric Green, *Represent*, March/April 2005

"Picking Myself Up," By Anita Ames, *YCteen*, November 2008

"Afraid to Learn," By Omar Morales, *YCteen*, December 1997

"Sticking With Your 'Own Kind,'" By Cassandra Thadal, *YCteen*, April 1998

"Getting Guys Off My Back," By Artiqua Steed, *YCteen*, April 1996

"Black Girl, White School," By Angelina Darrisaw, *YCteen*, September/October 2002

"Dropout Blues," By Diana Moreno, *YCteen*, December 1998

"When Great Isn't Good Enough," By Janill Briones, *YCteen*, September/October 2003

"They Called Me a 'Crack Baby,'" By Antwaun Garcia, *Represent*, March/April 2004

"The Suburbs: A Different World," By Dean Torres, *YCteen*, December 1998

"Real Smart," By Amber Grof, *Represent*, September/October 2008

"A School Where I Can Be Myself," By Wilber Valenzuela, *YCteen*, December 1992

"No More Hand Holding," By Edgar Lopez, *YCteen*, September/October 2008

"How I Graduated," By Angi Baptiste, *Represent*, May/June 1996

"Lost in a Big School," By Danica Webb, *Represent*, Spring 2012

"What's Wrong With Reading," By Anthony Turner, www.representmag.org, Oct. 2011

"You're On Your Own, Kid," By Otis Hampton, *Represent*, Spring 2012

About Youth Communication

Youth Communication's mission is to help marginalized youth develop their full potential through reading and writing, so that they can succeed in school and at work and contribute to their communities.

We publish true stories by teens that are developed in a rigorous writing program. These stories are uniquely compelling to peers who do not see their experiences reflected in mainstream reading materials. They motivate teens to read and write, encourage good values, and show teens how to make positive changes in their lives. For teachers and other staff, our materials and training provide tools to understand and engage hard-to-reach teens while helping them improve their academic, social, and emotional skills.

Our work is grounded in the belief that reading and writing remain the best ways to stimulate the imagination and to encourage reflection and discussion. We believe that literate, thoughtful citizens are essential to the survival of a vibrant, democratic society.

About The Editors

Al Desetta has been an editor of Youth Communication's two teen magazines, *Foster Care Youth United* (now known as *Represent*) and *New Youth Connections*. He was also an instructor in Youth Communication's juvenile prison writing program. In 1991, he became the organization's first director of teacher development, working with high school teachers to help them produce better writers and student publications.

Prior to working at Youth Communication, Desetta directed environmental education projects in New York City public high schools and worked as a reporter.

He has a master's degree in English literature from City College of the City University of New York and a bachelor's degree from the State University of New York at Binghamton, and he was a Revson Fellow at Columbia University for the 1990-91 academic year.

He is the editor of many books, including several other Youth Communication anthologies: *The Heart Knows Something Different: Teenage Voices from the Foster Care System*, *The Struggle to Be Strong*, and *The Courage to Be Yourself*. He is currently a freelance editor.

Keith Hefner co-founded Youth Communication in 1980 and has directed it ever since. He is the recipient of the Luther P. Jackson Education Award from the New York Association of Black Journalists and a MacArthur Fellowship. He was also a Revson Fellow at Columbia University.

Laura Longhine is the editorial director at Youth Communication. She edited *Represent*, Youth Communication's magazine by and for youth in foster care, for three years, and has written for a variety of publications. She has a BA in English from Tufts University and an MS in Journalism from Columbia University.

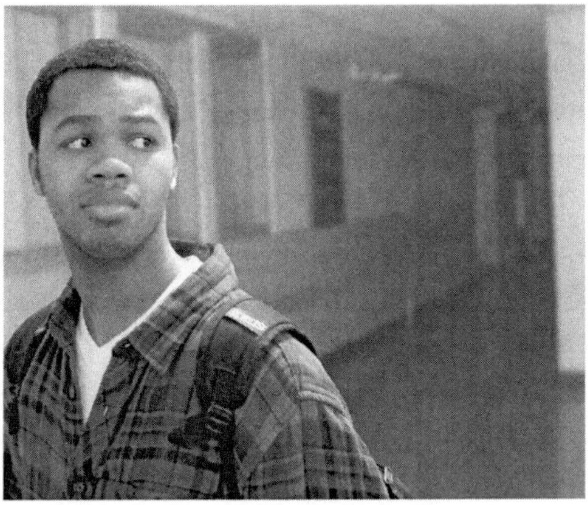

More Helpful Books From Youth Comunication

The Struggle to Be Strong: True Stories by Teens About Overcoming Tough Times. Foreword by Veronica Chambers. Help young people identify and build on their own strengths with 30 personal stories about resiliency. (Free Spirit)

Starting With "I": Personal Stories by Teenagers. "Who am I and who do I want to become?" Thirty-five stories examine this question through the lens of race, ethnicity, gender, sexuality, family, and more. Increase this book's value with the free Teacher's Guide, available from youthcomm.org. (Youth Communication)

Real Stories, Real Teens. Inspire teens to read and recognize their strengths with this collection of 26 true stories by teens. The young writers describe how they overcame significant challenges and stayed true to themselves. Also includes the first chapters from three novels in the Bluford Series. (Youth Communication)

The Courage to Be Yourself: True Stories by Teens About Cliques, Conflicts, and Overcoming Peer Pressure. In 26 first-person stories, teens write about their lives with searing honesty. These stories will inspire young readers to reflect on their own lives, work through their problems, and help them discover who they really are. (Free Spirit)

Out With It: Gay and Straight Teens Write About Homosexuality. Break stereotypes and provide support with this unflinching look at gay life from a teen's perspective. With a focus on urban youth, this book also includes several heterosexual teens' transformative experiences with gay peers. (Youth Communication)

Things Get Hectic: Teens Write About the Violence That Surrounds Them. Violence is commonplace in many teens' lives, be it bullying, gangs, dating, or family relationships. Hear the experiences of victims, perpetrators, and witnesses through more than 50 real-world stories. (Youth Communication)

My Secret Addiction: Teens Write About Cutting. These true accounts of cutting, or self-mutilation, offer a window into the personal and family situations that lead to this secret habit, and show how teens can get the help they need. (Youth Communication)

Sticks and Stones: Teens Write About Bullying. Shed light on bullying, as told from the perspectives of the perpetrator, the victim, and the witness. These stories show why bullying occurs, the harm it causes, and how it might be prevented. (Youth Communication)

Boys to Men: Teens Write About Becoming a Man. The young men in this book write about their confusion, ideals, and the challenges of becoming a man. Their honesty and courage make them role models for teens who are bombarded with contradictory messages about what it means to be a man. (Youth Communication)

Through Thick and Thin: Teens Write About Obesity, Eating Disorders and Self Image. Help teens who struggle with obesity, eating disorders and body weight issues. These stories show the pressures teens face when they are confronted by unrealistic standards for physical appearance, and how emotions can affect the way we eat. (Youth Communication)

To order these and other books, go to:
www.youthcomm.org
or call 212-279-0708 x115

Y 155.51825 FROM

From dropout to achiever

NWEST

R4000544711

Discard

NORTHWEST
Atlanta-Fulton Public Library

CPSIA
at www
Printed
FFOW0
8955FF